# FOCUS *on* FITNESS

# FOCUS *on* FITNESS

## Be Strong, Be Steady, Be Fit *and* Ready

# Russ D. Rhodes with Jo Ann Rhodes

XULON PRESS

Xulon Press
2301 Lucien Way #415
Maitland, FL 32751
407.339.4217
www.xulonpress.com

Printed in the United States of America

Paperback ISBN-13: 978-1-66281-549-2
Ebook ISBN-13: 978-1-66281-550-8

# Dedication

To the praise and glory of God

To our family and friends for their encouragement

To my father, Ralph D. Rhodes, who loved words,
loved the Word of the Lord
and
loved the Lord of the Word

# TABLE OF CONTENTS

# INTRODUCTION

Fitness is an important topic for people who want to improve their lifestyle while maintaining their physical and mental well-being. The average person wants to be able to enjoy work and play alike and that means finding the balance between the two.

Professional athletes have found a way to maintain their physical and mental well-being as they pursue their goal in the athletic arena. Their experience gives us some solid principles for keeping ourselves in good physical condition. Although by virtue of their pursuit of professional athleticism they take each principle to a higher level than necessary for the average person, the principles are valuable for everyone.

Professional athletes train regularly and often. Most work out and practice their skills five to six hours a day, six days a week, and close to 365 days a year. Their training requires both dedication and hard work. They are motivated by their desire to not only succeed in their sport, but to excel in it. Because of that dedication, they treat every practice like the actual event in which they will participate. Their eye is on the prize of being in the winner's circle.

Professional athletes work hard on their training, which is a well-rounded regimen of building strength and endurance, improving their skills, building confidence in their chosen field, and gaining a better knowledge of their body's abilities as well as their sport.

The Apostle Paul found athletes to be a fitting example of how we should approach our spiritual lives. We have a need to be fit spiritually if we want to live a strong Christ-like and Christ-centered life while here on earth. In 1 Timothy 4:7-8, Paul tells Timothy to "train yourself to be godly, for physical training is of some value, but godliness has value for all things, holding promise for both the present life and the life to come."

How does a Jesus-follower accomplish the goal of being godly? How can we be disciplined enough to finish our earthly lives victoriously? Our task is clear. We must recognize the value of following the example of the professional athletes' physical training principles and apply those same principles to our spiritual lives. In the words of Paul as found in 1 Corinthians 9:24-27 we find how to accomplish that. "Do you not know that in a race all the runners run, but only one gets the prize? Run in such a way as to get the prize. Everyone who competes in the games goes into strict training. They do it to get a crown that will not last, but we do it to get a crown that will last forever. Therefore I do not run like someone running aimlessly; I do not fight like a boxer beating the air. No, I strike a blow to my body and make it my slave so that after I have preached to others, I myself will not be disqualified for the prize."

It is imperative that we become strong and knowledgeable about our spiritual lives. We set our spiritual goals to know God and to follow Christ in every area of our lives, and then we begin training ourselves to be godly, just as Paul told Timothy to do. We develop discipline in our devotional and prayer life. We practice our spiritual skills of reading the Word of God, praying, and serving our Savior however we are able. As we practice, we grow stronger, become more fit spiritually.

Spiritual fitness creates in us a keener sense of our goal as individual followers of God. For the author of the poems found in this book, the development of spiritual fitness brought about the understanding of his goals as a poet:

## MY MISSION AS A WORDSMITH

Perfecting (maturing and strengthening)
The saints who are

Working (laboring in love)
In ministry to be

Edifying (building and outfitting)
The body of Christ

The poems and devotional thoughts included in this book are intended to be a resource for further training in your spiritual fitness routines. Their purpose is to be accessories to the main textbook of training, the Bible itself. They are for your FOCUS ON FITNESS.

# SECTION

*1*

## Train Yourself for Godliness

"Whoever serves me must follow me, and where I am, my servant also will be. My Father will honor the one who serves me." — John 12:26

# 1
# A SERVANT'S PRAYER

To serve God is
To follow Christ Jesus
God the Son

To serve God is
To know the presence of
God the Spirit

To serve God is
To enjoy the honor of
God the Father

Lord, may I serve You with
Regular Renewal
Constant Commitment
Daily Devotion and a
Forever Focus

Lord, may I serve You more
Faithfully
Enthusiastically
Consistently and
Joyfully

Lord, may I serve You and
Follow Your footsteps
Know Your presence and
Enjoy Your honor
Amen and Amen

*John 12:26*

# 2
# ALWAYS LET HIM LEAD

Always let Him lead you
　　Always let Him lead and
He will clear the road
　　For you to follow

*Proverbs 3:6*

# 3
# AS YOU GO

*As thou goest step by step*
*I will open up the way*
*before thee. Prov.4:12*
(old Hebrew translation)

As you go, step by step
I will open up
The way before you
I will open up the way

As you pray, day by day
I will open up
The way before you
I will open up the way

As you walk, trust and obey
I will open up
The way before you
I will open up the way

As you serve Him everyday
He will open up
The way before you

He will open up the way

# 4
# ASK SEEK KNOCK

Ask what ye will and to you it shall be given
Ask according to His will and He hears from heaven
Ask in prayer believing and receive ye surely shall
Ask and ye shall receive that your joy may be full

Seek ye first the Kingdom of God
Seek ye the Lord while He may be found
Seek the presence of the God of love
Seek those things that are above

Knock and God will open the door
Knock and God will give more and more
Knock for the Father is listening today
Knock and Jesus will show you the way

Keep getting to know God more and more
Keep yourself unspotted from the world
Keep on asking, knocking, seeking
Keep on keeping on keeping

A-Attitude of Attention
S-Silent Solitude
K-Knowing God

# 5
# BE READY

Be on your guard, be alert, be ready
Stand firm in the faith with a walk that's steady

Be alert, be ready
Stand firm and steady
Be brave, be strong
Be ready and steady your whole life long

Be men of courage, be brave, be strong
Be ready and steady your whole life long

If you wanna fight the Devil any time anywhere
Be much in the Bible and be much in prayer

I'm on my guard, I'm alert and ready
Standing firm in the faith with a walk that's steady

Yes I wanna fight the Devil any time anywhere
So I'm much in the Bible and I'm much in prayer

I'm alert, I'm ready
Standing firm and steady
I'm brave and strong
I'm ready and steady the whole day long

*1 Corinthians 16:13*

# 6
# BE THANKFUL

Be careful for nothing
    In nothing be anxious, my friend
In everything give thanks, In everything give thanks
    For this is God's will in Christ Jesus

Be thankful He hears you
    In nothing be doubtful, my friend

He hears and He answers, He hears and He answers

For this is God's promise and this is His plan

Be grateful He gave you
　　His Spirit to comfort and guide

He never will leave you, He never will leave you
　　Forever He will walk by your side

Be joyful, be joyful
　　The joy of the Lord is your strength

Sing and rejoice, give thanks and sing
　　Let us give praise to the King of Kings

Be thankful, be thankful, be thankful my friend
Be thankful, be thankful again and again

*Philippians 4:6*

# 7
# BE WILLING

Willing to send His Son to earth
Willing to offer His best for man
Willing to see the manger birth
Willing to go to Bethlehem

Willing to watch the lad grow up
Willing to let Him take His stand
Willing for Him to take the cup
Willing for Him to die for man

Willing for the shame and the cross
Willing to bear alone my sin
Willing for Him to suffer loss
Willing my pardon to begin

Willing to die my soul to save
Willing on my behalf to plead
Willing to rise up from the grave
Willing now to intercede

Willing not that any should perish
Willing that all may to Him come
Willing that they and I might cherish
Willingly the Heavenly Home

Willing the Good News to share
Willing to let the whole world know
Willing to tell folk everywhere
Willing His love to others show

# 8
# BEFORE THE CROWN

Before the crown we wear
We have a cross to bear
We have the Christ to share
We have a God Who cares
We see the worldly fare
We hear the devil's snares
We see the devil's flares
We know the devil scares
We see the need for prayers
We keep alert, aware
We fight the fight in pairs
We do not stop and stare
We have what God prepares
We have a home up there
We have a resting chair
We have a crown to wear

*Galatians 2:20*

# 9
# BUMPS, BURDENS AND BLESSINGS

**Bumps**: we all get them, don't like them but need them to keep us humble. They sure do remind us of just how frail we creatures of the earth really are. Like the cars we own, if we drive them as they were intended, rather then keep them in cold storage, there will be that inevitable bump, ding or scrape. We too, will have that chance bump, bruise or ding along the way of life, if we get out of cold storage and are doing the work we have been called to do. Let's not be like the fellow with a brand new Plymouth Fury who bemoaned the day he bought it when he discovered a nick in the door just two weeks later.

**Burdens**: we all have them, don't like them but need them to keep us depending on the Lord.
They also tend to draw us together if we are bearing one another's burdens. If we did not have our own burdens to bear we might think more highly of ourselves than we ought to think. Growing taller instead of growing deeper. Bearing burdens, especially those that belong to other folk, can be just the exercise needed to make us stronger.

**Blessing**: we all get them, don't deserve them but receive them so we will praise the Lord.
Yes, they are a part of God's loving care. Frequently they are the result of our bumps and burdens. Maybe it is like this: Bumps + Burdens = Blessings. God can use anything and everything to stretch us, strengthen us and grow us to become more and more like Him. We just have to be willing to be stretched, bumped, bruised and burdened. Then, God will pour out the barrels of His blessings, heaped up, pressed down and running over.

# 10
# BURDENS AND BLESSINGS

Burdens can become blessings
Trials turned into triumph
Thorns can bring thanksgiving

Burdens thorns and trials
Come from the trusted treasure chest of
God's wise and wonderful will

*2 Corinthians 12:7-10*

# 11
# CELEBRATING

Celebrating the land of the free
And the home of the brave
Celebrating our freedom in Christ
And his power to save

# 12
# COME UNTO ME

Come unto me for rest, renewal,
        restoration and revival
Come unto me for peace, purpose
        and power in ministry
Come unto me for forgiveness
        and reconciliation in relationships
Come unto me for safety and security
        in My sovereign will
Come unto me for provision and
        pleasure in My presence
Come unto me for faith and victory
        to overcome the world
Come unto me for joy all
        along the journey

Jesus says, "Come unto me
        And I will give you
            Myself to be

All that you need
And more."

# 13
# CRY UNTO GOD

Cry unto God and He will answer
    He will answer me

God will turn my enemies backward
    He will turn them back

This I know that God is for me
    He is there for me

*Psalm 56:9*

# 14
# ENJOYING ENLARGEMENT

V.1: Thou hast enlarged me when I was in distress
    I will be in distress
    God's *process* for growth
ENLARGEMENT -- stretching
    I will be stretched

V.7: Thou hast put gladness in my heart
    I will be glad of heart
    God's *provision* for joy
ENJOYMENT-- rejoicing
    I will be glad

V.8: Thou…makest me dwell in safety
    I will sleep in safety
    God's *protection* for life

CONTENTMENT-- resting
  I will be safe

*Psalm 4:1-8*

## 15
## EVERY MINUTE OF THE DAY

Every minute of the day
Every inch of the way
God holds your hand
And helps you stand
As you travel on
To the Promised Land

Every second of time
As you make your climb
Thru the valley deep
Or the mountain steep
God holds your hand
And guides your feet

Every day of the year
As the time draws near
Toward your heavenly home
No longer to roam
Seeing Christ the King
On His glorious throne

## 16
## EXPECTANTLY

I am the Lord,
The God of all mankind.
Is anything too hard for Me?

Thus saith the Lord,
The God Who is so kind,
There is nothing too hard for Me!

God keeps His word.
He never lags behind.
There is nothing too hard for Thee!

Can this be?
Wait and see
Expectantly.

*Jeremiah 32:27*

# 17
# FERVENT IN SPIRIT

Fervent in spirit, serving the Lord
    Walking in truth, obeying His word
Gratefully sharing day by day
    Faithfully witnessing, pointing the way

Fervent in spirit, serving the Lord
    Sowing the seed, planting the word
Praying that others, like Him shall be
    Bearing fruit for eternity

# 18
# FIT 2 ADD

Add wisdom to your heart
And sweetness to your lips
Adds learning to your life
Adds honey to your soul
And health to your bones

O Lord my Lord
Add wisdom to my heart
And sweetness to my lips

*Proverbs 16:23*

## 18a
# A BROKEN YOKE

### Leviticus 26:13b
*I broke the bars of your yoke and enabled you to
walk with heads held high.*

A yoke is burdensome not only by restricting an animal's freedom of move-
ment, but also by the heavy load it puts on their shoulders. Although a
yoke helps carry a heavy load, when a person uses a yoke to carry that load,
there are times when he can barely stand up straight with that yoke on his
shoulders.

When God breaks the burdensome yoke I am bearing as He speaks of in
this verse from the book of Leviticus, I can stand up straight and hold my
head up high. Whatever burdens weighed me down, whatever my past
might include, He removes the cause of shame or discouragement. My yoke
is broken and I am able to accomplish all of what God wants to do in me
and through me. I can carry a heavy load because my yoke is a unique one
provided by God.

Jesus Himself said in Matthew 11:30, "For my yoke is easy and my burden
is light." With Jesus in my life I am able to walk with my head held high
because His new yoke is not burdensome or humiliating. It grows strength
in me and it helps me stay on the right road and go in the right direction
no matter what kind of burden it includes. I have a wonderful Savior and
salvation. I can serve God better with my new yoke. I am training myself
for godliness.

# 19
# FIT 2 ADVANCE

ADVANCE in holiness
In love and faith
ADVANCE in righteousness
In hope and grace
ADVANCE in faithfulness

*Ephesians 4:15*

# 20
# FIT 2 ASK

Don't ask for more
Than you're willing to get
The children of Joseph wanted it all
More land more room and yet
Were not willing to work
They lost their get up and go
Their duties they did shirk
It was so it was slow

Don't ask for more
Than you're willing to share
Work and watch and pray
The Lord may return today
To the work I must go
Without delay to show
The world by what I say
That Christ the Lord loves them so

*Joshua 17:14-15*

# 21
## FIT 2 B

Chosen royal peculiar priestly
And beloved of God
What manner of persons
Ought we to be
And walk as saints have trod

*1 Peter 2:9*

# 22
## FIT 2 B A GOOD MAN

He loves training and discipline
Obtains God's favor
Unmoved
Crowned with an excellent wife
Just in thought
Speaks persuasively

Stable
Insightful
Compassionate
Hard working
Fruitful
Escapes trouble

Satisfied with what he says
Listens to advice
Conceals dishonor
Truthful
His words bring healing
Established

Peaceful and joyful

Delights God
Hides knowledge
Works diligently
Has gladness of heart
Guides his neighbor

Honors diligence and
Enjoys life

*Proverbs 12*

## 23
## FIT 2 B A GOOD WIFE

She is the most valuable treasure
A man can find
She can be trusted all of the time
She always does her husband good
She works with her hands with delight
She is thrifty and clever with food
She rises early caring for her family
She wisely buys and sells property

She is strong and confident
She stays up late preparing for tomorrow
She makes her own clothes
She generously helps the poor
She is always ready for the future
She makes and sells fine garments
She wears strength and dignity graciously

She smiles at the future
She speaks with wisdom
She teaches kindness
She looks out for her household
She is not idle

She is blessed by her children
She is praised by her husband
Who says
There are many good women
But you are the best
And because of you
I am so blessed

*Proverbs 31:10-31*

## 24
## FIT 2 B A HUMDINGER

The musical instrument of your life
Has only one short string to strum
So make sure it's a real humdinger
And its beautiful note is love
The end pegs that help make it a singer
Are prayer and a faith from above

## 25
## FIT 2 B A LEADER

Love to learn
Learn to lead
Lead to leave
A legacy

A good leader
Is always
A great learner

A poor leader
Is always
A sorry learner

Lord help me become
A life long learner

Lord help me
Love to learn
Learn to lead
Lead to leave
A legacy

# SECTION
## 2

### SET A GOAL

"Teach me to do your will, for you are my God;
may your good Spirit lead me on level ground."
— Psalm 143:10

## 26
## FIT 2 B A MAN

God must be first
Tell the truth
Be pure
Always

Go right the wrong
Sing your song
Stand tall
Always

## 27
## FIT 2 B A SERVANT

I am Your servant
I am in total darkness
I have given up hope
I remember what You did
I lift up my hands in prayer
I thirst for water from You

I feel hopeless
I want to learn more about Your love
I trust You
I come to You in prayer
I ask You to guide me
I come to You for safety

I want You to show me what to do
I want You to lead me
I ask You to keep me safe
I ask You to protect me from trouble
I want You to destroy my enemies
I am Your servant

As His servant
Be humble before God
Be honest with God
Be honored by God

*Psalm 143*

## 28
## FIT 2 B @ JESUS' FEET

At the feet of Jesus
That's where I like to be
At the feet of Jesus
That's the place for me

At the feet of Jesus
Quiet sure repose
At the feet of Jesus
My soul lives and grows

At the feet of Jesus
Comfort in my grief
At the feet of Jesus
Finding full relief

At the feet of Jesus
He my sorrow shares
At the feet of Jesus
He my burden bears

At the feet of Jesus
He gives peace and rest
At the feet of Jesus
I am truly blessed

## 29
## FIT 2 B BLESSED (10x)

1. You Lord bless everyone who lives right
2. You bless all who depend on You for strength
3. You bless all who deeply desire your presence
4. Your people grow stronger
5. Your work will be seen
6. You shield and protect Your people
7. You are like the sun and shield
8. You treat us with kindness and honor
9. You deny nothing from those who live right
10. You bless everyone who trusts You

So: Live right. Be strong. Stay close
God works. God protects. God shows
God honors. God gives. God blesses

*Psalm 84*

## 30
## FIT 2 B BOLD

Come boldly
Obtain mercy
And find grace
In time of need

Ask largely
Expectantly
See His face
He hears you plead

Now draw near
He sees your tear
Just keep pace

He's sure to lead

Find His grace
See His face
Just keep pace

*Hebrews 4:16*

# 31
# FIT 2 B BOLD AND B HOLD

To behold His dear face
To be told of His grace
To be bold anyplace

# 32
# FIT 2 B BUILDING

Be Building
Yourselves now up
On your holy faith

Be Praying
In the Spirit
Each and every day

Be Keeping
Yourselves in step
With the love of God

Be Looking
For His mercy
On the road you trod

Be Helping

Just any one
Who may have doubts and fears

Be Rescuing
All those who
Need saving from the fires

*Jude 1:20-23*

# 33
# FIT 2 B COMPLETE IN HIM

His knowledge our instruction
His wisdom our direction
His power our protection
His love our consolation

His mercy our comfort
His grace our salvation
His justice our surety
His promise our hope

His holiness our utmost
His hands our confidence
His heart our assurance
His word our trust

His faithfulness our triumph
His plan our purpose
His will our pleasure
His glory our ambition
His presence our joy

*Colossians 2:10*

# 34
## FIT 2 B CONTINUALLY

Continually with God
Continually upon His mind
Continually before His eyes

Continually in His hand
Continually on His heart
Continually in His love

Continually in His care
Continually in His favor
Continually He is here

*Psalm 73:23*

# 35
## FIT 2 B DELIGHTING GOD

Knowing God comes before
Asking God
Seeking God comes before
Serving God
Understanding God comes before
Following God
Hearing God speak comes before
Speaking with God
Watching God work comes before
Working with God

Knowing seeking understanding God
Is the way to be delighting God

*Jeremiah 9:23-24*

# 36
# FIT 2 B FILLED

O Lord may I truly

Be filled with the knowledge of Your will
Be walking in a manner worthy of the Lord
Be bearing fruit in every good work
Be increasing in the knowledge of God
Be strengthened with all power
Be attaining all steadfastness
Be joyously giving thanks

Be filled
Be humble
Be fruitful
Helps in knowing God better
Knowing God better helps to
Be strong
Be steady
Be thankful

*Colossians 1:9-12*


# 36a
# BE CAREFUL

**Deuteronomy 8:11**
*Take care lest you forget the Lord your God by not keeping his
commandments and his rules and his statutes.*

Be careful. We understand that principle well because we have heard it since
the first time we took a step as a toddler. We use that phrase frequently as
adults. Be careful when you cross the street. Be careful when you drive. Be
careful to eat right. Every time we use the phrase "be careful" we understand
the implication that there is some kind of danger that we must be alert to.

Deuteronomy 8:11 tells us that this principle is no different in our spiritual lives. We face an inherent danger if we do not stay close to God and His principles of living. We will forget God if we do not "take care."

Be careful to read God's Word. Be careful to obey His commands and His leading. Be careful to stay in touch with Him through prayer. Be careful to serve Him with your whole heart, mind and strength.

If we are not careful, it will be a matter of *when* we forget God not *if* we forget, so be careful. We need to set our goal to be careful.

## 37
## FIT 2 B FULL

The fatness of thy house
The fountain of full life
The river of thy pleasure
The brightness of thy light

How excellent how excellent
Thy lovingkindness O God

*Psalm 36:8*

## 38
## FIT 2 B GOING

Where you came from
Is not that important
Where you are going
Really is
Look where you are going
Go where you are looking

Look to Jesus He knows best

Look to Jesus and find rest
Look to Jesus as He pleads
Look to Jesus as He leads

Go to Jesus he'll forgive
Go to Jesus now and live
Go to Jesus for His power
Go to Jesus hour by hour

## 39
## FIT 2 B HIS

I was in His mind
From eternity
I was in His heart
On Mount Calvary

I am in His prayer
As He intercedes
I am in His care
As He guides and leads
I am in His arms
Where He comforts me
I am in His will
Where He gives me peace
I am in His work
Where He gives increase
I am in His love
Where joys never cease

I was in Your mind
From eternity
I was in Your heart
On Mount Calvary

# 40
## FIT 2 B HIS SHEEP

He calls us
He leads us
He restores us

He owns us
He rescues us
He protects us

He rejoices over us
He gives us life
He died for us
He keeps us

Thank You Lord
For being our Shepherd
And we are
Your weak and humble sheep

*John 10:1-29*

# 41
## FIT 2 B HOLY

When holy in the day so bright
Then happy in the darkest night
When holy on the highest hill
Then happy in the deepest well
When holy with my friends all near
Then happy as they disappear
When holy as the Lord has said
Then happy on my dying bed

## 42
## FIT 2 B HOLINESS EXPRESSED

The walking of my feet
The talking of my tongue
The thinking of my mind
The work my hands have done
Must be scrutinized
By the eyes
Of God and Christ the Son
For you see
His plan for me
Is holiness
Experienced
And expressed

*I Peter 1:16*

## 43
## FIT 2 B IN GOD

In God I will praise His word
In God I have put my trust
In God I will never fear
In God is the strength of my life
In God is my salvation and light
In God is my comfort and stay
In God is my joy every day

*Psalm 56:3-4*
*Psalm 27:1*

# 44
# FIT 2 B JOYFUL

Be joyful
Be prayerful
Be thankful
In every situation
In every circumstance
In every way every day

Joy makes your pathway bright
Prayer brings down heavenly light
Thanks changes the darkest night

Sing with gladness
Pray when sadness
Overwhelms your soul
Give thanks and sing
For it will bring
God's warmth when you are cold

*1 Thessalonians 5:14-18*

# 45
# FIT 2 B KEPT

LORD keep me:

Keep me headed in the right direction
Keep me learning to live and love
Keep me centered on God the Father
Keep me committed to the Great Commission
Keep me focused on spiritual fitness

Keep me determined to be disciplined
Keep me running the race to win

Keep me praying for power in prayer
Keep me working to win the lost
Keep me practicing the presence of Christ

# 46
# FIT 2 B KING

O Lord You are God alone

You are great
You are mighty in power
You are King of the Nations

O Lord there is none like You

You are the true God
You are the living God
You are the Everlasting King

O Lord in power You made the earth

You in wisdom establish the world
You in understanding stretch out the heavens
You speak and the earth quakes

O Lord You cause the clouds to ascend

You made the lightning for the rain
You bring wind from your storehouses
You do it again and again

O Lord You alone are KING

*Jeremiah 10:6-13*

# 47
# FIT 2 B KNOWN

Known of God completely (v.1-6)
My ups and downs
My all arounds
My thoughts and words
Behind before
Known of God completely

Known of God continually (v.7-12)
In heaven or hell
He there doth dwell
If winged to the sea
He there doth lead
In darkest night
He's there with light
Known of God continually

Known of God compassionately (v.13-18)
Formed from above
Knit together in love
Wonderfully made
Framed up my way
Ordained all my days
He's worthy of praise
Precious indeed
Thy thoughts unto me
As sand by the sea
When I awake
I am still with thee
Known of God compassionately

*Psalm 139:1-18*

# 48
# FIT 2 B LIKE JESUS

He has been with Jesus
He's been taught of Him
He's becoming like Him
In His boldness
Loving-kindness
And forgiveness

He's becoming like Jesus
In His prayerfulness
In His steadfastness
In His holiness
He is zealous
He has been with Jesus

*Acts 4:13*

# 49
# FIT 2 B LISTENING

Listen with you heart open
And your mouth closed

Listen with your eyes up
And your knees down

Listen with your mind active
And your feet still

# 50
# FIT 2 B LOOKING

Look where you're going

Or
Go where you're looking
I told our daughter
Learning
A bike to ride

Today I say
Look where God's going
Then
Go where God's looking
That's the way to stay
Close by His side

# 51
# FIT 2 B LOOKING INTO

LOOKING into the past:
Blessings from the Lord
Protection on the way
Instruction in the Word
Provision every day

LOOKING into the present:
Vision with a cost
Inspiration too
Compassion for the lost
Strength for work to do

Pressing toward the goal
Holding forth the light
Reaching one last soul
Fighting the good fight

LOOKING into the future:
Hearing soon Well Done
Finishing the race

Seeing Christ the Son
In glory face to face

# 52
# FIT 2 B MASTER-WORKS

Men who are the Master-works of God are:

Men who stand up in difficulties
Men who stand steadfast in tests
Men who stand strong in the battle
Men who stand unmovable
Men who stand confident of victory
Men who stand true in trials
Men who stand trusting God above all
Men who stand tall for the truth
Men who stand believing God in prayer
Men who keep on standing

And having done all to stand
O Lord may I be such a man

*Ephesians 6:13*

# 53
# FIT 2 B MEEK

The meek
Will He teach His way
The meek
Will He bless each day
Be teachable
Be blessable
Seek to be meek

*Psalm 25:9*

# 54
# FIT 2 B MORE

If we were more alone with God
We would all know more of God
We would live more near to God
We would grow more in grace
We would walk more by faith
We would trust and obey more
And become more like the Lord
Whom we worship and adore

*Genesis 24:63*

# 54a
# NOT JUST A SNACK

**Psalm 22:26**
*The afflicted [the poor (NIV)] shall eat and be satisfied,
those who seek him shall praise the Lord!*

Experts tell us that one of the main principles for good nutrition is eating the right kinds of foods. When a person eats a well-balanced diet, not only do they stay healthy, but they also find satisfaction in what they eat because the food is answering the basic cravings and nutritional needs of the body. In order to be healthy, we must set our goal for how many calories we will eat as well as what kind of food it will be.

This verse from Psalm twenty-two tells us that the same principle is true regarding spiritual food. True and complete spiritual satisfaction will only come when we eat nutritional spiritual food. Seeking the Lord, even when troubled ("afflicted", "poor"), is what will bring true satisfaction to our hearts and souls.

This verse and psalm appear just before the well-known and much-loved Psalm 23, which talks about satisfaction. It is as though the psalmist is describing the satisfaction that comes from spiritual eating and being satisfied. Look at all the ways satisfaction is described in Psalm 23. The author says "I shall not want" (v.2). He follows that expression of satisfaction with "I will fear no evil" (v.4), and "my cup overflows" (v.5). There is true, filling satisfaction when we eat nutritional spiritual food, rather than just a snack. Eating it will give us the nutrition – and the enjoyment – we need for healthy living. Set your goal to eat more than just a snack.

## 55
## FIT 2 B MOVED

Move me God
Anywhere on life's checkerboard
Plant me God
Anywhere in life's garden

Ready to go
Ready to stay
Ready to sow
Along the way

# SECTION
## *3*

### USE SELF DISCIPLINE

"Rejoice always, pray continually, and give thanks in all circumstances, for this is God's will for you in Christ Jesus. Do not quench the Spirit ... hold on to what is good, reject every kind of evil."
— 1 Thessalonians 5:16-22

## 56
## FIT 2 B PEACEFUL

Be joyful be peaceful
Be thankful all the time
This is God's holy will for you
And it brings peace of mind

Put not out the Spirit's fire
Test everything hold to the good
Avoid every kind of evil desire
Just do the things you know you should

*1 Thessalonians 5:16-22*

## 57
## FIT 2 B PEACEFUL AND PRAYERFUL

Be joyful
    Rejoice in hope
Be peaceful
    Patient in trouble
Be prayerful
    Constant in prayer

*Romans 12:12*

## 58
## FIT 2 B QUICK

Quick to praise God
Slow to criticize Him
Quick to thank God
Slow to question Him

Quick to follow
Slow to wander
Quick to serve Him
Slow to squander

Quick to love Him
Slow to leave Him
Quick to obey
Slow to go astray

Quick to glorify
Slow to wonder why
Quick to listen
Slow to speak
Quick to turn
The other cheek

*James 1:19*

# 59
# FIT 2 B QUIET

In the madness
Quiet my soul
In the sadness
Make me whole
In the confusion
Guide me on
In the confession
Make me one
In the night time
Be my stay
In the bright time
Lead the way

# 60
# FIT 2 B READY

Toes pointed in a heavenly direction
Hands folded for a heavenly connection
Tongue ready for a heavenly inspection
Mind ready for a heavenly correction
Soul ready for a heavenly injection
Body ready for heavenly protection

# 61
# FIT 2 B RESTING

Resting Reflecting
Refreshing Renewing
Rekindling Rejoicing

The road to rejoicing
Always starts with resting

# 62
# FIT 2 B RESTORED

Bask in the sunshine of God's
Love each day
Pause in the peaceful presence
Of the Lord
Feed in His green pastures
On the way
Rest by the quiet waters and
Be restored

*Psalm 23*

## 63
## FIT 2 B RIGHT

Walk right
Work right
Talk right
Praise right
Honor right
Get right
Give right
Be rock solid right

*Psalm 15*

## 64
## FIT 2 B ROOTED

Be rooted and grounded in love
Be filled with the fullness of God
Be able to comprehend with all saints
The breadth and length and depth and height
And to know the great love of Christ

Be rooted and grounded
Be living and giving
Be ready and steady
Be growing and showing
His love from above

*Ephesians 3:17-19*

## 65
## FIT 2 B SAVIOR

Unchanging Savior

Undying love
Undeserved favor
Unending mercy

Untarnished testimony
Unthinkable miracles
Unbelievable forgiveness
Untouchable holiness

Unimaginable splendor
Unflinching focus
Unconventional talk
Unblemished walk
Unalterable teaching
Unforgettable preaching

This Christ Jesus the Lord
Is my Savior forever
According to His word

## 66
## FIT 2 B SEASONED

### SEASONED SENIORS

Salty and crusty
Or worn out and rusty
Peppered with spice
Or naughty or nice

Sometimes so sweet
But not always neat
Candy cane plain
Or using the cane

Seasoned from above

With a heavenly love
Seasoned here below
With a Christ like glow

Buttery talker
Or using a walker
Cinnamon topping
Or time to be stopping
For rest with the best

Was that wise beyond years
Or prized among peers
The choice will be ours
To be sweet or be sour

Seasoned from above
With a heavenly love
Seasoned here below
With a Christ like glow

## 67
## FIT 2 B SILENCED

LORD
In Your presence
I am silenced
In Your power
I am preserved
In Your arms
I am comforted
In Your hands
I am molded

LORD
In Your will
I am blessed

In Your eyes
I am righteous
In Your heart
I am loved
In Your presence
I am silenced
Amen and amen

# 68
# FIT 2 B STEADY

Serve with charity
Fulfill your ministry
Teach with clarity
Always be steady
Always be ready

*2 Timothy 4:5*

# 69
# FIT 2 B STILL

Be still and know
That I am God
Be still I'll show
The open road
Be still and grow
To be like Me
Be still and glow
For all to see

# 70
## FIT 2 B STRONG

God is my hope and strength
God is with me in trouble
God is here to help right early

God speaks, the earth melts
God is with me as my refuge
God stops wars, breaks bows,
Snaps spears and burns chariots

Therefore I should stop to listen
And learn that God is God alone
God will be exalted among the heathen
God of hosts is with me as my refuge

*Psalm 46*

# 71
## FIT 2 B TRIED

God knoweth the way that I take
When He hath tried me
I shall come forth as gold
I shall come forth as gold
Why should I ever forsake
He's always beside me
I believe what He told
I shall come forth as gold

*Job 23:10*

# 72
## FIT 2 B TRIED AND WIN

These are the times that try
But not the time to cry

We must be AUTHENTIC – In difficult times
our neighbors, family and friends see what
we are really made of, from beginning to end.

We must have a GREATER LOVE FOR GOD –
A heart full of love, no matter how we try,
always spills over to those nearby.

We must have a WILLINGNESS TO SUFFER –
Christ taught us how to suffer. How well did
we learn, my brother?

We must have a WILLINGNESS TO SERVE –
Jesus said he came to serve and washed his
disciples feet. Are we serving God and others
or do we just retreat?

We must RELY MORE ON PRAYER – God
always answers every prayer; sometimes yes,
sometimes no, just because He loves us so.
Sometimes He says wait, but He is never late.

We must HAVE REAL COMMUNITY – Work
together, pray together, share together and stay
together like godly glue for me and you. Let the
outside pressure melt us together as one in the Lord.

We must REMAIN PURE AND TRUE – God
only uses those who have clean hands and a
pure heart to serve, honor and worship Him.

We must BE RESPONSIBLE – Mean what we
say and say what we mean. Keeping our word
and doing what we promise is key.

We must keep the MAIN THING the MAIN
THING – Focus on what really matters, the
eternal stuff and not the other fluff.

We must remember the HOLY SPIRIT ALWAYS
MAKES A WAY – God delights in doing the
impossible for His glory alone. He is still on
the throne.

We must remember the LOCAL CHURCH IS
MORE IMPORTANT THAN EVER – It was
His plan and still is His plan. So get with the
plan, O man!

# 72a
# JUST FLIP THE SWITCH TO "ON"

### Psalm 29:11
*The Lord gives strength to his people; the Lord blesses his people with peace.*

One of the electrical outlets in our house needed repair. It would not hold
a plug tightly enough. Consequently, whenever I used that outlet to plug
in my vacuum cleaner, it would take only a slight extra tug on the plug for
it to come out and the vacuum cleaner would suddenly come to a stop.
The vacuum cleaner worked fine, but only when it was plugged into the
outlet properly.

I think of my outlet and vacuum cleaner when I read this verse from Psalm
29. Did you notice that this verse does not say that strength and peace are
*available* to God's people? It says they *have* those two spiritual commodities.
When I am God's child I do not have to ask the Lord for strength or for peace.
They are already in me to put to use. I received them as soon as I trusted in

Christ as my Savior. This is a profound truth that many of us who are God's children often miss when faced with life's challenges. We frequently ask the Lord for strength or for peace when we should actually be asking the Lord to help us *use* them. I should be asking God to help me learn to put them to use, to appropriate their power in my circumstances, whatever those circumstances may be at any given time. It is like using my plugged in vacuum cleaner. The power is already in the electric lines coming into the house but if my outlet is not working well or my vacuum cleaner is not staying plugged in, that electricity is of no value to me for vacuuming my carpet.

All I have to do is have the vacuum cleaner plugged into an outlet, turn the switch to "on" and the power is mine to use. Discipline yourself to stay plugged in.

# 73
# FIT 2 B WATCHFUL

Because God is great I am grateful
Because God is good I am thankful
Because God is here I am joyful
Because God is there I am hopeful

Because God is loving I am prayerful
Because God is holy I am careful
Because God is giving I am faithful
Because God is living I am fruitful

Because God is sovereign I am mindful
Because God is just I am thoughtful
Because God is worthy I am worshipful
Because God is caring I am peaceful

Because God is captain I am respectful
Because God is mighty I am restful
Because God is winning I am cheerful
Because God is coming I am watchful

# 74
# FIT 2 B WISE

A wise man:

Will hear Be listening
Will learn Be learning
Will increase Be growing
Will understand Be caring
Will attain Be maturing

*Proverbs 1:5*

# 75
# FIT 2 B WISE AND KNOW

Wisdom is
Knowing what to overlook
And what to look over

Wisdom is
Not just in the things you choose
But also in the things you don't choose

Wisdom is
Not just going across the sea
But seeing the cross in me

Wisdom is
Not just in the things you do
But also in the things you don't do

Wisdom is
Not just planning where you want to flourish
But flourishing in the place God plants you

Wisdom is
Not just enriching your own life
But enriching the lives of others

Wisdom is
Making your goal a ready start
Toward a loving heart and a restful soul

Lord make me wise beyond my years
And make me wise beyond my fears

*Psalm 37:30-31*

# 76
## FIT 2 BE BROKEN

Most younger men today
Are like unbroken stallions
God get off my back
And don't keep track
Don't tell me
What to do
No one tells me
What to do
I can do
As I please
Never bow my knees
I am accountable to no one
But me myself and I
And I can make it on my own

# 77
# FIT 2 BE DIFFERENT

## DARE TO BE DIFFERENT

Dare to be like Joseph
Dare to stand alone
Dare to dream big dreams for God
Dare to make them known

Dare to pray like Daniel
Dare to pray out loud
Dare to pray three times a day
Dare to trust in God

Dare to live like Caleb
Dare to follow right
Dare to do what honors God
Dare to take the mountain height

Dare to live like David
With a tender heart
Confessed whenever he was wrong
And got a fresh new start

Dare to be like Abraham
A man of faith was he
Who trusted God and not in man
And went obediently

# 78
# FIT 2 BE DONE
# (A Prayer for Help)

Lord please
Give me work
Until my life is done
And Lord
Give me life
Until my work is done

Lord please
Give me help
As I help others
And Lord
Give me others
Who really need my help
Amen

# SECTION
## 4

## WALK REGULARLY

"If we walk in the light, as he is in the light, we have
fellowship with one another, and the blood of Jesus,
His Son, purifies us from all sin." — 1 John 1:7

# 79
# FIT 2 BE FIT

Stay fit
Stay focused
Stay fighting
Stay faithful

Stay fit to be useful
Stay focused on the eternal
Stay fighting the battle
Stay faithful

# 80
# FIT 2 BEE PLEASING

BEE PLEASING THE LORD

Bee loving—as a Christian Brother (v.1)
Bee hospitable—to neighbors and strangers (v.2)
Bee empathetic—to prisoners and persecuted (v,3)
Bee pure and honorable—in your marriage (v.4)
Bee free—of the love of money (v.5)
Bee content—with what you have (v.5)
Bee confident—in the Lord (v.6)
Bee not fearful—of man (v.6)

*Hebrews 13:1-6*

# 81
# FIT 2 BEHOLD

Beholding Christ we are
Becoming like the Lord
Reflecting His image we are

Glorifying the Lord

*2 Corinthians 3:18*

## 82
## FIT 2 BEND

I am a wee bit feeble
My eyes are growing dim
I'm losing a little hearing
My hands have lost their grip

My legs are not as strong
My balance comes and goes
I can't go all day long
I have the senior woes

But Lord this is my plea
And may it ever be
I lift my prayers to thee
Give thanks on bended knee

Let my knees always bend
And all my prayers ascend
To God who reigns above
Blessing me with His love

## 83
## FIT 2 BEND LOW

Slow down to grow up
Go deep to grow tall
Bend low to go high

Go slower
Bend lower
Go deeper

Go slower
Grow taller
Go higher

# 84
# FIT 2 BIND UP

God will
Seek that which was lost
Bring back the driven
Bind up the broken
The sick He will strengthen

*Exodus.34:16*

# 85
# FIT 2 BLESS

Bless the Lord:

All His hosts
All His works
O my soul
Lute and harp
Horn and dance
Cymbals too
Flute and strings
Trumpet sound
Sun and moon
Starry host
Rocks and stones

Flowers and trees
Angelic beings

*Psalm 103:21-22*
*Psalm 150*

# 86
# FIT 2 BRING

The LORD has power

To bring big accomplishments
From small beginnings

To bring a great journey
From first steps

To bring large harvests
From tiny seeds

To bring grand results
From two mites

To bring big answers
From little prayers

To bring great joy
From deep sorrow

To bring about beauty
From gray ashes

To bring strong hope
From weak faith

To bring men alive
From the dead

## 87
## FIT 2 BRING IN

Out of death into life
Out of darkness into light
Out of blindness into sight
Out of despair into delight

Out of selfish ambition
Into heavenly expectation
Out of noisy agitation
Into quiet meditation

Out of destruction into restoration
Out of rebellion into revival
Out of criticizing into harmonizing
Out of doing more into being more

Out of prideful thinking
Into humble serving
Out of carnal living
Into sacrificial giving

Out of getting more stuff
Into having more time
Out of spiritual poverty
Into heavenly wealth

Out of rampant remorse
Into royal reward
Out of sorrow and sadness
Into jubilant gladness

He brought us out that
He might bring us in.

*Deuteronomy 6:23*

# 88
# FIT 2 BUILD

Building Blocks of Biblical Love
    Jesus as the Foundation of Love

Block 1: Knowledge and discernment (v.9)
    Psalm 40:8; 119:70
    2 Corinthians 5:14-15, John 14:15

Block 2: Life approving excellent things (v.10)
    Philippians 1:27
    Ephesians 5:10, Hebrews 12

Block 3: Lifestyle blameless, pure, and sincere
    Judged by the light
    Hebrews 4:13, Philippians 2:15

The Mortar keeping it together (v.11)
    Fruit of righteousness
    Galatians 5:20 – love, joy, peace…

*Philippians 1:8*

# 89
# FIT 2 C HEAVEN

HEAVEN:
The Celestial City of God
The community of saints abode

The place of peace
The presence of Christ

The focus on Him

The absence of sin
The sermon is done
The victory won

The need of no light
The place without night
The tearless treasurer
The glory beyond measure

The start of eternity
The end of all pain for me
The pleasure at His right hand
The joyful triumphant band

The sound of singing
The praises ringing
Around the throne of
The KING of kings

The blessed home of the believers
The community of humility
The reward of the redeemed
The palace of the persevering

The destiny of His disciples
The prize of the persistent
The goal of the godly
The dwelling of the doers of the Word

The timeless place
Of His marvelous grace
Where we look upon
His glorious face

# 90
# FIT 2 CALL

Call to me
Out of duty
Out of discipline
Out of desire
Out of desperation
Out of delight

*Psalm 145:17ff*

# 90a
# DO NOT CORRODE YOURSELF

### Psalm 37:1, 7, 8
*Fret not yourself*

The Grand Canyon is an awe-inspiring example of the corrosive power of water against rock. The Colorado River, after flowing through the mountain range for many years, has worn the rock down to the point that at some places the Grand Canyon is a mile deep.

In Psalm 37, the phrase "fret not yourself" is repeated three times, so it must have some significance for the reader. To fret means to feel worry, annoyance or discontent. Interestingly, the word also means to cause corrosion like water does over stones in a stream. I am told to not fret myself, to not feel worry or annoyance over evil doers (v.1). I often need that reminder when I listen to local, national, or international newscasts. The world is full of opportunities to feel fretful if I allow myself do so.

I should not cause myself corrosion or agitation because it only causes harm to myself (v.8 says it tends only to evil). Whatever I allow myself to fret over causes me no benefit and in fact, it causes only harm. And the very phrase "fret not yourself" tells me this is something I must work to manage within my own mind and heart. I can choose whether or not to fret. I can choose whether or not to worry. I can choose whether or not to corrode myself. I can choose to get worn down by circumstances, or I can choose to put my faith and trust in God.

In Matthew 7:25, Jesus tells us, "Do not worry about your life, what you will eat or drink, or about your body, what you will wear." He follows up on that by saying, in verses 33-34, "But seek first his kingdom and his righteousness, and all these things will be given to you as well. Therefore do not worry about tomorrow." In other words, do not fret (and corrode) yourself. Walk without worry.

# 91
## FIT 2 CALL UPON THE LORD

Call upon the Lord
Who says in His Word
I will answer you
I will be with you
I will deliver you
I will honor you
I will satisfy you
Therefore give Him praise
Through out all your days

*Psalm 91:15*

# SECTION
## 5

## RUN WITH PERSEVERANCE

"Therefore, since we are surrounded by such a great cloud of witnesses, let us throw off everything that hinders and the sin that so easily entangles. And let us run with perseverance the race marked out for us."
— Hebrews 12:1

## 92
## FIT 2 CHANGE MY HEART

Change my heart O Lord
Renew my mind in the Word
Bless my hands in the work
Direct my feet in your way

## 93
## FIT 2 CHANGE

Yesterday we cannot undo
But what we do today 'tis true
Can bring change tomorrow for you

## 94
## FIT 2 CHOOSE

O my brothers sisters friends
Few serve well
Serve well to the end
May it be said
Be said of you
You chose to be among the few

## 95
## FIT 2 CLIMB THE LADDER OF LOVE

LOVE
BROTHERLY KINDNESS
GODLINESS
STEADFASTNESS
SELF- CONTROL
KNOWLEDGE

VIRTUE
FAITH

*2 Peter 1:5-7*

2 FAITH
+
2 VIRTUE
+
2 KNOWLEDGE
+
2 SELF-CONTROL
+
2 STEADFASTNESS
+
2 GODLINESS
+
2 BROTHERLY KINDNESS
 +
LOVE

If you practice these qualities you will never fall
*2 Peter 1:10b*


# 96
# FIT 2 CLIMB

Climbin' up the mountain chil'ren
Take jus' one step at a time
Climbin' up the mountain chil'ren
The view up there is sublime

Climbin' up the mountain chil'ren
God is here to guide you every day
Climbin' up the mountain chil'ren
He will hold your hand all the way

Climbin' up the mountain
Climbin' up slow
Climbin' up the mountain
That's the way to grow

Climbin' up the mountain chil'ren
Keep your feet steady and be strong
Climbin' up the mountain chil'ren
Always be ready with a song

Climbin' up the mountain chil'ren
Serve one another on the road
Climbin' up the mountain chil'ren
Help your brother with his load

Climbin' up the mountain
Higher every day
Climbin' up the mountain
Singin' all the way

# 97
# FIT 2 COME STAY GO

Boldly come to the throne of God
Humbly stay in the presence of God
Faithfully go in the power of God

*Hebrews 4:16*

# 98
# FIT 2 CONSIDER

Consider now
The wonder of His birth
The wonder of His life

The wonder of His love
The wonder of His death
The wonder of the cross
He came as a babe
To country folk
Not to those with a crown
Nor to those of the cloth

## 99
## FIT 2 COUNT

Count your many burdens
Name them two by two
Then you'll see that others
Have problems just like you

Count your many blessings
Name them one by one
Clouds may hide God's blessing
As they do the sun

Count your many blessings
Name them four by four
It will not surprise you
God has far more in store

## 100
## FIT 2 CREATE

God the Great Creator

Starting time for all creation
Blending mud to make a man
Blanketing the cosmos with stars
Separating the seas from land

Painting colored flowers everywhere
Placing us in His tender care
Ordering the seasons one-by-one
Providing salvation through His Son
Giving us joy along our journey
Granting us peace for every day
Offering rest for all the weary
Guarding and guiding us all the way

# 101
# FIT 2 DECLARE

I have not hid
Thy righteousness
I have declared
Thy faithfulness
I have not concealed
Thy lovingkindness

*Psalm 40:10*

# 102
# FIT 2 DELIVER

Hear me O Lord
Show me thy face
Tell me each morn
Show me the way
Deliver me
Hide me I pray
Teach me to please thee
Quicken today

*Psalm 143:7-11*

## 103
## FIT 2 DELIVER AND DELIGHT

Thy WORD gives me understanding
Thy WORD gives me deliverance
And perseverance
Thy WORD gives me a song all day long
Thy WORD gives me help
Thy WORD gives me instruction
And correction
Thy WORD gives me delight even in the night
Thy WORD gives me guidance
Thy WORD gives me life

*Psalm 119:169-176*

## 104
## FIT 2 DIE YOUNG

LORD
Let me keep dreaming big dreams
Until my life is gone
Let my imagination outrun
My memory with a song
And at a very old age
O Lord, let me die young

## 105
## FIT 2 DO NOW

Procrastination saps your power
Completion brings success
DO IT NOW this very hour

(I'll finish this last line later.)

Better still you fill it in
And send it back to me
I'll publish one or two of them
As quick as might can be

# 106
# FIT 2 DO ABUNDANTLY

GOD IS ABLE

Able to do exceedingly abundantly
Able to make all grace abound
Able to save them to the uttermost
Able to keep you from falling
Able to deliver us
Able to keep what I have committed
Able to subdue all things unto Himself

*2 Timothy 1:12*

# 107
# FIT 2 DO LOVE AND WALK

Do justly
Love mercy
Walk humbly

Do the right thing
Love the right stuff
Walk the right way

Doing what is good
Loving what is better
Walking with the best

Doing what is righteous
Loving what is holy
Walking with the lowly

Doing what's right thru God
Loving the mercy of God
Walking humbly with God

*Micah 6:8*

# 108
# FIT 2 DO RIGHT

Do what is right
Love what is good
Humble yourself
To walk with God

*Micah 6:8*

# 108a
# NEW YORK-STYLE CHEESECAKE

### Psalm 63:5
*I will be fully satisfied as with the richest of foods; with
singing lips my mouth will praise you.*

One of my favorite desserts is a slice of a plain New York style cheesecake;
no added toppings, just cheesecake. The delight for me is not just in the
flavor, but with the indulgent, rich, smooth, creamy texture that fills my
mouth and the lingering taste that coats my tongue. I always hate to see
that flavor and consistency go away when I drink something or brush my
teeth after eating.

That cheesecake delight is what I think of when I read this verse. It reminds me of the satisfaction that the Bible tells us comes only from God. Only the knowledge and experience of seeing God meet the needs of our hearts can give us true and lasting satisfaction. Jesus alone can fulfill the desires of our hearts. Only a relationship with God through Jesus will put an end to our need and desire for love and acceptance. Only God's Holy Spirit can give us assurance of salvation and right standing with God. Only God, through His Word can dispel our doubts sufficiently.

Satisfaction from a relationship with God and His Word results in praise. Praise is one of our ways to express the joy that satisfaction brings. Praise brings my spirit into tune with God's Spirit and in doing so I find a deep and rich satisfaction that is unlike any other satisfying experience. In His coming to earth that first Christmas day, Jesus provided us with the means to find satisfaction and that satisfaction is what gives us joy that lasts much longer than a helping of cheesecake. Run with satisfaction, peace and perseverance.

# 109
# FIT 2 DREAM

Dream big dreams for God
Do great things for God
Give your days to God
Give your praise to God

# 110
# FIT 2 ENJOY HEAVEN

As citizens of heaven

We enjoy the GOVERNMENT of heaven

Where God is:
Supreme Sovereign of all

Owner and Orchestrator
Maker and Manager
Ruler and Regulator
Leader and Lord
Proper Proprietor

Where we:
Gratefully receive His decrees
Orders and proclamations
Obey and do cheerfully
His will without hesitation

We enjoy the HONORS of heaven

We are:
Sons of God
Joint heirs with Christ
Comforted by the Spirit
Guided by God
Provided His presence
Granted His glory
Served by angels
Companions with saints
Crowned with immortality

We enjoy the PROPERTY of heaven

A Heavenly Home
A Crown of Righteousness
A Crown of Life
A Robe of Righteousness
The Gates of Pearl
The Azure Lights of the city
The River of the Water of Life

We enjoy the DELIGHTS of heaven

No Night there for
The Lamb is the Light
To be like Him
To see Him as He is
No more sickness or sadness
No more tears no more fears
No more sighs or goodbyes
No more death or decay
No more hunger or thirst
No desire to be first
No trials or temptations
No faithless frustrations
No more time constraints
No misery or complaints
No more worries or war
No more pressure or pain
No more loss only gain
No more struggles or strife
No more loneliness in life
No more selfishness
A sinless environment

We enjoy MORE DELIGHTS of heaven

Twelve manner of Fruits Forever
Angelic Choirs singing
David's Orchestra playing
Worshipping God forever
Learning more of God's character
Rejoicing when sinners repent
Going wherever we're sent
Seeing Jesus face-to-face
Singing the Glories of His Grace
Casting our crowns at Jesus' feet
Charmed with His smile very sweet
Eating the Marriage Supper of the Lamb
Fellowshipping with the Great I AM

As citizens of heaven
Let us live like our
High Heavenly
Dignity Demands

*Ephesians 2:19*

## 111
## FIT 2 FADE AWAY

Once Mom's steps were strong
And her stride was long
As she walked with the Lord each day

But now she quakes
With each step she takes
As we walk along the way

We pray for grace
As we learn to face
That she's slowly fading away

Yes we're losing our mother
Little by little and like no other
She has less and less to say

Her mind was sharp and very strong
But now it's going and almost gone
As she slowly fades away

We miss you Mom really miss you
The loving mother that we knew
But that's OK as we trust and pray
For the Lord to carry us thru
As you slowly fade away

## 112
## FIT 2 FEED AND FOLLOW

You are to feed your soul
God will follow your situation
You run to reach the goal
God will bring you His salvation

Following faithfully the Heavenly Father
Keeping step with the Holy Spirit
Joining hands on the job with Jesus

*Colossians 3:1-3*

## 113
## FIT 2 FIGHT

Fight
Fight hard
Fight hard now
Fight hard now as a man
Fight hard now as a man of God
F – Focus on forever finding time for
    Family friends and godly fellowship
    (FAITHFULNESS)
I – Intensify your devotion to God
    Your family and your church
    (INTEGRITY)
G – Go deeper into God's Word
    Grow stronger like the Lord
    (GODLINESS)
H – Hone your healthy habits
    Hunger to know God
    (HUMILITY)
T – Take time to be holy
    Tell others your story

To God be the glory
(TRUTHFULNESS)

# 114
# FIT 2 FIGHT THE GOOD FIGHT

Sit in God's presence and be still
Kneel in surrender to His will
Rest in His peaceful arms of love
Stand with His power from above
Walk with the Lord every day
Fight the good fight come what may

# 115
# FIT 2 FILL UP

Sit up - sooner
Get up - quicker
Stand up - straighter

Show up - eager
Listen up - better
Study up - harder

Fill up - fuller
Grow up - stronger
Speak up - longer

*2 Timothy 2:15*

## 116
## FIT 2 FINISH WELL

Beginning well is good
Running well is better
Setting out is good
Holding out is best
Starting well is fine
Finishing well sublime

# SECTION
## 6

# STRENGTHEN YOUR
# HEART AND MUSCLES

"Let us draw near to God with a sincere heart
and with the full assurance that faith brings."
— Hebrews 10:22

# 117
# FIT 2 FOCUS

A broken heart
A worshiping heart
Surrendered to God
A giving heart
Giving ourselves
Waiting then going

"Get our hearts right"
Hold fast with a
Position of
Focused
Attention

*Hebrews 10:19-25*
*Philippians 2:15-16*

# 118
# FIT 2 FOCUS 10X

Focus on the Master
Not the ministry

Focus on the Savior
Not the service you do

Focus on the Spirit
Not your sphere of influence

Focus on the Father
Not his followers

Focus on just listening
Not great learning

Focus on the Who
Not the why

Focus on His presence
Not His power

Focus on His peace
Not His provision

Focus on just Him
Not your sin

Focus on the Word
Not the world

## 119
## FIT 2 FOLLOW, FIT 2 LEAD

Caleb was a leader
The battles he did win
By challenging his men
His daughter followed on
In the example left by him

First be a great follower
Then be a great observer
Next be a great leader
Then be a great encourager
Finally be a great winner

Follow
Observe
Lead
Encourage
Win

*Joshua 15:14-19*

## 120
## FIT 2 FORGE AHEAD

Work smarter
Play harder
Rest better

Pray longer
Sing louder
Speak softer

Obey quickly
Serve faithfully
Give generously

Reach higher
Focus further
Do things greater

Ask more
Seek more
Find more

Look forward
Look outward
Look upward

Forget the past
Fight on in the present
Forge ahead toward the prize

# 121
# FIT 2 GIVE YOURSELF

Giving is what makes a life
It makes a life worth living
Give yourself to others first
Giving yourself away is best

Give your ears
Give your tears
Give your cheers

Give your prayers
Give a hand
Understand their cares
Give a smile
Walk with them a while

Giving makes a life worth living
Give yourself away
Giving gives and keeps on giving
Give yourself today

# 122
# FIT 2 GO 2 COLLEGE

The College of Contentment

Content
In poverty or in wealth
In sickness or in health
To have or not to have
Yes
Contentment must be learned
Learning must be disciplined
Discipline must be desired

Desire must be divine
For
Godliness is a means of
Great gain and reward
When accompanied by
Learned contentment from
Jesus Christ the LORD

*Philippians 4:11*
*I Timothy 6:6*

# 123
# FIT 2 GO

Go up higher
    With your walk with the Lord
Go down deeper
    As you study His good Word
Go out further
    With the gospel that you share
Go on longer
    Showing love that you really care
Go ye into
    All the world and preach - Mark 16:15
Go work harder
    Telling forth your story
Go sing louder
    Giving God the glory

*Mark 16:15*

# 124
# FIT 2 GO WITH GOD

Go with the Wind of the Holy Spirit
Stand with those who stand tall
Wait for the Word when God is in it
Give your best give it all

Work with a passion while it is day
Pray like you really mean it
Press on no matter what folks say
Fight for you know God will win it

Guard your mind your mouth your heart
Keep your sword sharp and ready
Do your best always right from the start
Walk with God strong and steady

Go with God
Reach His goal

# 125
# FIT 2 GO NOW

Go where you're sent
Grow where you're planted
Show what you meant
Finish what you started

Go thru those doors
Just keep on going
Always look for more
Ways to be sowing

Go don't look back
Focus on God's glory

Please don't get slack
In telling The Ol' Story

Go and make disciples
Following His command
Be a living epistle
All across the land

Go where you're sent
Go thru those doors
Go don't look back
Go look for more

*Matthew 28:19-20*

# 126
# FIT 2 GO ON

From strength to strength
From glory to glory
From place to place
From top to bottom
From here to there
From cold to hot

# 126a
# BE LIKE RAIN FALLING

### Psalm 72:6
*May he be like rain falling on a mown field,*
*like showers watering the earth.*

Have you ever noticed how refreshing the outdoors seems to be after it rains? Sometimes it seems you can almost hear the grass groaning with delight. There are days when you can see the flowers standing taller and the leaves on the bushes lifting themselves after rain has fallen.

What a lovely way to describe the kind of person people like to be around. A person pleasant to be with, one who makes you feel refreshed when you leave their presence. A person like that leaves a benefit from their presence. They enrich the lives of those around them. Their "rain" refreshes those in their presence. Who would not want to be that kind of person? That is God's design for each of His children.

## 127
## FIT 2 GO THE RIGHT WAY
## FIT 2 DO THE RIGHT THING

Dad told me when I would disobey
And punish me the very same day
Your action hurts me more than you know
And it hurts the Lord even more
Please don't do this anymore

Another saying my Dad had was
Only one life t'will soon be past
Only what's done for Christ will last
I've added some lines to make them rhyme

Tell out the Good News while it is day
Each one reach one and do not delay
People need the Lord and forgiveness
Let's make witnessing our business
Only what's done for Christ will last

St. Francis said it the very best yet
Preach every chance every chance you get
And once in a while you can use words
Just leave all the rest to the Lord

Only what's done for Christ will last

## 128
## FIT 2 GROW

Meditate day and night
In the Law of the Lord
Take your delight
In the most Holy Word

*Psalm 1:2*

## 129
## FIT 2 GROW BY FAITH

Faith grows
As we feed on God's Holy Word
Faith grows
As we obey God's perfect will
Faith grows
As we feed on God's faithfulness
Faith grows
As we take time just to be still

## 130
## FIT 2 GROW IN VISION

Lord Please Let
The words of my mouth
The thoughts of my mind
The meditation of my heart
The direction of my feet
The work of my hands

Be acceptable in Your sight

Lord Please Let
The love of my life
The thirst of my soul
The vision of my future
The focus of my faith
The purpose of my plans

Be acceptable in Your sight

*Psalm 139*

## 131
## FIT 2 GROW UP

Keep low
That's God's humble plan
Look up
View His nail scarred hands
Press on
To the Promised Land

Keep low Look up Press on
Become like Christ the Son
Press on Look up Keep low
The only way to grow

## 132
## FIT 2 HATE

Thou hatest wickedness

Christ bled to wound it
Christ died to kill it

Christ was buried to bury it
Christ arose to trample it
Christ lives to oppose it

O Lord
May I learn to hate
The wickedness at my gate
The wickedness all around me
The wickedness found inside me

*Psalm 45:7*

# 133
# FIT 2 HAVE HOPE

My hope is in the Lord
My help comes from the Lord
My healing is according to the Lord

My happiness is confidence in the Lord
My hands are strengthened by the Lord
My house is open to the Lord

My heart is convicted by the Lord
My head is pillowed by the Lord
My honor is given to the Lord

*Psalm 146:5*

# 134
# FIT 2 HEAR

The sound of sheer silence
Is found in His presence
Where God speaks His mind

If we take the time
To listen in hushed
Surrender

So stop walking stop talking
Stop whining stop pining
Let God hold your tongue
As He shares His heart
So tender

# 135
# FIT 2 HEARKEN

Come and hearken
Keep thy tongue
Depart from evil
Do good everyone

Seek real peace
Pursue it now
Our God sees
And He hears
The righteous cry
The Lord is nigh

*Psalm 34:11-22*

# 136
# FIT 2 HOLD

Hold that fast
Which thou hast
That no man take thy crown

Fight the fight

With thy might
And take the higher ground

Do your job
Just for God
And give Him all the praise

Serve the Lord
Heed His word
Enjoy Him all thy days

*Revelation 3:11*

## 137
## FIT 2 HOLD FAST

Hold fast the word of life
Stay strong and brave and true
Obey and serve the Lord
In all you think and do

Hold forth the word of life
Stay faithful to the task
Teach preach and live the truth
Is all the Lord doth ask

*Philippians 2:16*

## 138
## FIT 2 HONOR DAD

Dad was my hero, coach and teacher
My pastor, friend and counselor
Administer of discipline
Judicator of justice

Keeper of the car keys

Dad was a giver of guidance
My leader and pathfinder
Provider and protector
Instructor of righteousness
Example of holiness

Glad to have had
Such a dad
Proud to be
Son number three

## 139
## FIT 2 IGNITE

Stir our hearts
Ignite the flame
Of our passion for more
Of you O Lord

Loosen our tongues
Take our hands
As we're holding forth
The Word of Life

Lead the way
Light the path
As we work and walk
With you O Lord

Stir Ignite
Loosen and Take
Lead with Light
The path that you make

*Psalm 23:2*
*Psalm 16:11*
*Psalm 77:19*

## 140
## FIT 2 KEEP NOT BACK

Keep not back
Your talents time and treasure
Use all for His good pleasure

Keep not back
Your abilities small or great
Use them all for heaven's sake

Keep not back
Your influences for good
And live for God as you should

Keep not back
Go forward to the fight
And serve Him day and night

Keep not back
Help others on the road
Help carry their big load

Keep not back
O soldier of the cross
Count not the heavy cost
And keep not back

*Isaiah 43:6*

# 141
# FIT 2 KNOW

Jesus knows me this I love
Jesus shows me all his care
Jesus guides me from above
Jesus hears my every prayer

Jesus knows me this I love
Jesus knows my burdens too
Jesus gives grace just enough
Jesus He will carry me through

Jesus knows me this I love
Jesus speaks His word to me
Jesus cares when the way is rough
Jesus meets my every need

Yes Jesus knows me
He knows me and He cares

# 142
# FIT 2 KNOW GOD'S BLESSING

The stream of God
Is full of water
The family of God
Shall be rejoicing
The city of God
Is full of laughter
The man of God
Shall know His blessing

*Psalm 65:9*

## 143
## FIT 2 KNOW GOD

God's grace in immeasurable
God's mercy is inexhaustible
God's peace in inexpressible
God's love is immutable
God's Son is indescribable
God's Spirit is invisible
God's person is inextricable
God's character is impeccable
God's power is incomprehensible
God's purpose is incontrovertible
God's judgment is inescapable
God's Word is infallible

*2 Timothy 1:2*

## 144
## FIT 2 LEAD

Warm my heart
All day long
Stir my soul
Make it strong
Fill my mind
Keep it pure
Make me whole
Steadfast sure

Lead my feet
In Your way
Bend my knees
Help me pray
Move my legs
Forward march

Push on me
Give me starch

# 144a
# REMARKABLE RIGHTEOUSNESS

### Psalm 112:6-8
*A righteous man will have no fear of bad news; his heart is steadfast,*
*trusting in the Lord. His heart is secure, he will have no fear.*

According to these verses in Psalm 112, if I am righteous (have a relation-ship with God through my faith in Christ as my Savior), the results are remarkable.

I will be *optimistic*. These verses say I will have no fear of bad news.

I will be *steady*. My heart will be steadfast – firm and unwavering – in the face of varying emotions or circumstances.

I will be *secure*. I trust in the Lord, so I am not fearful of all the imperfect things, people or experiences that come my way.

I will be *fearless*. Bad news and bad events will happen but God can keep me from being paralyzed by fear in the face of those things.

That is a remarkable righteousness to have. Strengthen your spiritual mus-cles for optimism, firmness, security and fearlessness.

# 145
# FIT 2 LEAD AND OBEY

Listen to the Word of God
Learn by obeying the truth of God
Look to the Guiding Spirit of God
Lean upon the power of God

Then
Lead others into the
    Purpose and presence of God

# SECTION
## 7

# DRINK PLENTY OF WATER

"To the thirsty I will give water without cost from the spring of the water of life." — Revelation 21:6

# 146
# FIT 2 LEARN

Learning:

To listen to the still small
    Voice of the Holy Spirit
To love the Lord
    As I ought to love
To lean on Jesus and not
    My own understanding
To look for new ways to
    Reach a lost world
To lead my family to worship
    And serve God faithfully
To lay all my burdens
    At the feet of Jesus
To lift my voice in praise
    Seven times each day

# 147
# FIT 2 LISTEN LOOK AND LEARN

Listen to what God says
Look at what God does
Learn just who God is

# 148
# FIT 2 LEARN A LOT

Moses learned a lot
In the palace of the king
He learned a whole lot more
In the desert of the King of kings

Jonah learned a lot
As a prophet with a wish
He learned a whole lot more
In the belly of a fish

Samson learned a lot
As a Nazarite he scorned
He learned a whole lot more
As he was grinding out the corn

Peter learned a lot
And he wanted more to know
He learned a whole lot more
When he heard the rooster crow

Martha learned a lot
Working cooking serving meat
Mary learned a whole lot more
Sitting still at Jesus' feet

In the desert of the Lord
Or the belly of a whale
Maybe grinding out the corn
It is best just to be still

## 149
## FIT 2 LISTEN 2 THE LORD

Be quiet for a while
Turn the Bible on
Choose the right frequency
Tune in carefully
Crank up the volume
Open up the Word
Avoid interruptive static
Stay on the station

Document your discovery
Determine to obey

# 150
## FIT 2 LISTEN WHEN GOD SPEAKS

When God speaks
Big things happen

The sea roars
Thunder echoes above
His powerful voice
Is full of majesty
His voice is
Mighty and marvelous

Cedar trees are
Destroyed and shattered
Mountains skip
Like a calf and
Jump like a wild ox

The lightning flashes
Shivers and shakes
Deer give birth early
Trees are stripped of leaves
Oak trees are twisted around

Everyone shouts His praise
God rules on His throne forever
He will make us strong
He will give us peace

When God speaks
Big things happen
When God speaks

I will listen

*Psalm 29*

## 151
## FIT 2 LISTEN AND HEAR

Turn off the radio
Turn off the stereo
Turn off the TV
And listen to Me

God is speaking
Are you listening?

Listen to the birds singing
Hear the frogs burping
Listen to the geese honking
Hear the dogs barking

Listen to the wind howling
Hear the leaves rustling
Listen to the trees humming
Hear the rain dropping

Listen to the cows mooing
Hear the crickets chirping
Listen to the doves cooing
Hear the cat slurping

Hear the sounds
All around

Listen to the children crying
Hear the parents shouting
Listen to the neighbors fussing
Hear the plumber cussing

Listen to the beggar begging
Hear the seller hawking
Listen to the buyers bragging
Hear the people nagging

Listen to the workers gripping
Hear the sinners sighing
All his friends are dying

God is speaking
Are you listening?

*Isaiah 1:2-3*

## 152
## FIT 2 LISTEN LEARN LOVE

Focus on God the Father
Submit to the Holy Spirit
In silence and solitude
Surrender to the Savior
Listen to the Lord and
Put your whole heart in it

## 153
## FIT 2 LOVE LISTEN LEARN LEAD

Love to learn
Love to learn to listen
Learn to listen in love

Learn to love by listening
Listen while you learn to love
Love while you learn to listen

Lead by loving to learn
Lead by learning to love
Lead by learning to listen

Lead only after you
Learn to
Listen in
Love to the Lord

## 154
## FIT 2 LIVE BY THE SPIRIT

Live by the Spirit
Led by the Spirit

Walk by the Spirit
Work by the Spirit

## 155
## FIT 2 LIVE

I will put on the full armor of God
I will fight the good fight of Faith
I will pray always with all prayer and supplication
I will walk and live by faith alone

I will go in the strength of the Lord God
I will not fear what man can do unto me
I will fear God only and serve Him joyfully
I will love the Lord with all my heart,
    mind, soul and strength

## 156
## FIT 2 LIVE AGAIN

He came a babe to Bethlehem
He came to bring peace on the earth
He came to bring Good News to men
He came to give us second birth

He lived to do God's Holy will
He lived to heal the sick and lame
He lived the Scriptures to fulfill
He lived to save that's why He came

He died a sinless sacrifice
He died for all the world to see
He died to save and give us life
He died alone for you and me

He lives to draw us to God The King
He lives for us to intercede
He lives that we might live again
He lives to meet us in our need

He came He lived
He bled for man
He died He rose
He lives again

## 157
## FIT 2 LIVE FAITHFULLY

Let what you do
And what you say
Bring glory to
The Lord always

In righteousness
In holiness
In blessedness
You live

In faithfulness
In gentleness
In fruitfulness
You give

May what I do
And what I say
Bring glory to
The Lord always

In righteousness
In holiness
In blessedness

I'll live

In faithfulness
In gentleness
In fruitfulness
I'll give

## 158
## FIT 2 LIVE AND LOVE

Live to please God
    More and more (v.1-2)
Love to help others
    More and more (v.9-10)
Lead a life
    Of quietness (v.11)
Look after
    What's yours (v.11)
Labor with
    Your own hands (v.11)
Leave a
    Godly example (v.12)
Lean on
    God alone (v.12)

*1 Thessalonians 4:1-12*

## 159
## FIT 2 LIVE BY FAITH

The just by faith shall live
They in God's presence be
They praise and thanks shall give
To God the One in Three

The just shall live by faith
This is what God hath said
Surrounded now by death
But God shall raise the dead

The just by faith shall live
They with the Lord shall run
The gospel message give
Until the race is won

*Habakkuk 2:4*

## 160
## FIT 2 LOOK 2 JESUS

Look off unto Jesus why worry and doubt
Look off unto Jesus and He'll bring you out

Look off unto Jesus there's no need to fear
Look off unto Jesus He surely is near

Look off unto Jesus and go not astray
Look off unto Jesus He shows you the way

Look off unto Jesus your spirit to bless
Look off unto Jesus in Him you'll find rest

Look off unto Jesus and gaze on His face
Look off unto Jesus you're here by His grace

## 161
## FIT 2 LOOK

LOOKING into the past:

Blessings from the Lord
Protection on the way
Instruction in the Word
Provision every day

LOOKING into the present:

Vision with a cost
Inspiration too
Compassion for the lost
Strength for work to do

Pressing toward the goal
Holding forth the light
Reaching one last soul
Fighting the good fight

LOOKING into the future:

Hearing soon well done
Finishing the race
Seeing Christ the Son
In glory face to face

# 162
# FIT 2 LOOK OUT

Look out
For the devil's on the loose
Look out
For he wants you in his noose

Look back
You have come by faith this far
Look back
And raise your Ebenezer

Look ahead
For the road is rough and steep
Look ahead
Yes, the trials make you sweet

Look on
Watch the Lord at work today
Look on
He's the Potter, you're the clay

Look up
Your redemption draweth near
Look up
You are closer by a year

## 162a
# EVERY LIVING THING

### Psalm 145:16
*You open your hand and satisfy the desires of every living thing.*

"Every living thing." This verse says God satisfies the desires of "every living thing," not just the desires of the hearts of human beings, but of *every living thing.* That is what God does for all of creation. He meets all their needs. That means that when it rains, God is satisfying the desire of the grass and trees and flowers. When flowers create nectar, God is satisfying the desire of the bees and the hummingbirds. When I put seeds in the birdfeeders God is using me to help provide for the satisfaction of the desires of the birds. He satisfies the desires of *every* living thing, even though that "desire" is of a different nature than mine as a human being, made in God's image.

Remember what Jesus Himself said in Matthew 6:26: "Look at the birds of the air; they do not sow or reap or store away in barns, and yet your heavenly Father feeds them. Are you not much more valuable than they?"

## 163
## FIT 2 LOOK BEYOND

Look beyond yesterday
And see His faithful Hand
Look beyond tomorrow
And see the Promised Land

*Psalm 106:12-15*

## 164
## FIT 2 LOVE LAUGH LIVE

Love a little
Laugh a little
Live a little

Love some more
Laugh some more
Live some more

Love a lot
Laugh a lot
Live a lot

*Psalm 97:11-12*

## 165
## FIT 2 MAKE HIM KNOWN

My hands are tired
My back is bent
My eyes are dim
My throat is sore
My mind is weak

My legs are limp
But my heart is full
And I will press on
To know Him and
To make Him known
This Jesus Christ
God's only Son


# 166
# FIT 2 MAKE MUSIC

God the Music Maker

The morning stars
Together are singing
As He rejoices
Over us with joy
Angels with their
Harps are bringing
Worship and praise
Without alloy

Some birds have
A single song
Others with variation
Mocking birds copy them
All day long
Catbirds call
Without hesitation

Dogs and squirrels
Bark their praise
Cats mostly offer
A quiet meow
But as for the cow
She just says mooo

So why oh why can't I
Sing His praises too?

Yes I will sing of my Redeemer
And His wondrous love for me
Sing hosanna sing hosanna
Hallelujah sing with me

# 167
# FIT 2 MARVEL

Marvelous are Your works O Lord
Merciful are Your ways
Majestic are You O Lord
Multiple are Your blessings

Magnificent is Your creation
Melodious is Your voice
Masterful is Your Word
Meticulous is Your care

Moderate is Your wrath
Memorable are Your miracles
Mysterious are Your paths
Of peace and power
Myriad are Your thoughts
Toward us each hour

# 168
# FIT 2 MEDITATE

I will remember
The days of old
I will meditate
On all Thy works

I will muse
On the works of Thy hand
I will remember
And not grow cold
I will remember
God understands
He has a plan
For every man

*Psalm 143:5*

## 169
## FIT 2 MEND

Lord mend me
And bend me
Then send me

Lord mend me and my heart
Bend me in every part
Send me with a fresh start

Lord mend me
And bend me
Then send me forth I pray
Lord mend me
And bend me
Then send me forth today

Lord mend me with Your love
Then bend me from above
And send me with a shove

Lord mend me and make me new
Bend and make me holy too
Send me forth to live like You

# 170
## FIT 2 MOVE OUT

Moving out in God's good will
Or sitting still in yours
Moving forward to the hill
Or sitting by the open doors

Moving out in God's good plan
Or sitting still with yours
Moving toward the Promised Land
Or sitting fearing distant shores

Moving out in God's strong hand
Or sitting on your own
Moving with the warrior band
Toward heaven's most glorious throne

Moving out in God's good will
Moving out in God's good plan
Moving out not sitting still
Moving out in God's strong hand

# 171
## FIT 2 OBEY

Just obedience
    Is a duty
Willing obedience
    Is a delight
Faithful obedience
    Is dependable
Loving obedience
    Is commendable

*Luke 17:10*

## 172
## FIT 2 OCCUPY (Work, Engage)

Occupy till I come
Christ gave the authority
To every man his work
To his several ability
That ye should follow His steps
Preach the word
Reprove rebuke exhort
With the kindness of the Lord
Every man's work
Shall be made manifest
Therefore be ye steadfast
Unmovable abounding
In the work of the Lord
For your laboring
Is not vain in the Lord

*Luke 19:13*
*1 Corinthians 15:58*

## 173
## FIT 2 ONLY BE

Only to be what God wants me to be
Every day as I walk His way
Only to do what God wants me to do
Only His will to obey

Only to say what God wants me to say
Others their burdens to bear
Only to give what God want me to give
To share and to offer a prayer

Only for Jesus I give Him my all

Only for Jesus to answer His call
Only for Jesus to run hard the race
Only for Jesus I'll soon see His face

## 174
## FIT 2 PAY ATTENTION

Learning to listen to the Lord
Paying attention to His
Still small voice
While working playing
Resting praying
Studying
Or just being still

## 175
## FIT 2 PLEASE GOD

Quick footed
Light heeled
Fast knees
Strong willed

Pace setter
Goal getter
High stepper
Straight runner

Forward looker
Wind catcher
Lean learner
Great gainer

Prize winner
Crown wearer

World changer
God pleaser

*2 Samuel 18:23*

## 176
## FIT 2 PRAY AND PRAISE

Prayer
The helper of our learning
Praise
The object of our growing
Prayer and Praise
The mix for our worshiping

## 177
## FIT 2 PRAISE

Tragedy turns to triumph
By the grace of God
Melody gives life meaning
On the road we trod

Harmony helps the healing
Through the love of God
Symphony brings together
Praise beneath the cloud

## 178
## FIT 2 PRAISE THE CHILD

A Child is born
A Son is given
A Man of Sorrows

A Savior dies
A Father knows

A Mighty God
A Risen Lord
A Counselor
A Prince of Peace
A Coming King

*Isaiah 9:6*

# 179
# FIT 2 PRAISE GOD

My Heavenly Father:

He creates
He sustains
He provides
He maintains
He loves
He cares
He forgives
He shares
He helps
He heals
He keeps
He seals

My Earthly Father:

He loved God
He served others
He preached the Word
He taught us how to live here
And how to get there

He walked and lived by faith
He stood tall and loved all
He worked and played hard
He loved a good story
And gave others the glory
He was the best dad
That I ever had

# 180
# FIT 2 PRAISE HIM

I will sing of Your Power
I will sing of Your Mercy
I will sing Your praises
I will sing Your praises

You have been my sure Defense
You have been my good Refuge
In the day of trouble
In the day of trouble

You have been my sure Defense
You have been my constant Strength
I will sing Your Praises
I will sing Your Praises

*Psalm 59:16*

# 180a
# ATHLETIC FAITH

## Psalm 147:10-11
*His pleasure is not in the strength of the horse, nor his delight in the legs of a man, the Lord delights in those who fear him, who put their hope in his unfailing love.*

Throughout history people have admired athletes. In our current society, we pay them higher wages than the majority of other wage-earners. People listen carefully to their opinions. They are held up as role models by many people, young and old alike. Most of us get delight from watching them perform in their athletic roles.

As important as athletes may appear to be in our society, the Lord finds much more pleasure in my simple faith and trust in Him. This is what He looks for in me, not for my strength to run or ability to jump, throw, dribble, or handle a ball, a bat, or a stick. For me, as un-athletic as I am, this is most comforting and encouraging. What the Lord wants from me is diligent, regular practice in fearing Him and putting my hope and trust in Him no matter what my circumstances may be. He wants athletic-style faith.

## 181
## FIT 2 PRAISE HIS NAME

His name is above every name
His name is as ointment poured forth
His name shall be called Wonderful
His name is excellent is all the earth

His name every knee should bow
His name is a strong tower
His name is very safe
His name is Counselor

His name is Mighty God
His name is glorious
His name is Prince of Peace
His name means God with us

# SECTION
## *8*

## BUILD FLEXIBILITY

"Forgetting what is behind and straining toward what
is ahead, I press on." — Philippians 3:13-14

# 182
# FIT 2 PRAY

Prayer is most often
Under attack from the enemy
Of the Lord and
Under utilized by the Army
Of the Lord

# 183
# FIT 2 PRAY AND SING

In the morning when I rise
You are there
When I open up my eyes
You are here
In the morning when I kneel
In humble prayer
In my heart O Lord I feel
You really care

In the noon time
When the skies are clear
And so bright
And I watch the
Shadows disappear
In the light
I still know that you are here
What delight

In the evening with the shadows
Deep and long
When the troubles of the day
Are almost gone
In the darkest of the night
And all alone

Then O Lord I praise you
With a song

*Psalm 88:13*
*Psalm 40:3*

## 184
## FIT 2 PRAY LIKE JABEZ

Bless me O Lord bless me indeed
And make me a blessing to those in need
Broaden my borders and ministry too
And may I bring great glory to You
Keep me from sin and evil snares
And thank You Lord for answered prayers

*1 Chronicles 4:10*

## 185
## FIT 2 PREACH

I run not uncertainly
I fight not aimlessly
I live not inconsistently
I preach not powerlessly

*1 Corinthians 9:25-27*

## 186
## FIT 2 PRESS ON

Every minute of the day
Every inch of the way
God holds your hand

And helps you stand
As you travel on
To the Promised Land

Minute second day of life
Soon will end the battle strife
Victory won through Christ the Son
But till then keep pressing on

Every second of time
As you make your climb
Thru the valley deep
Or the mountain steep
God holds your hand
And guides your feet

Every day of the year
As the time draws near
Toward your heavenly home
No longer to roam
Seeing Christ the King
On His glorious throne

# 187
# FIT 2 PRESS ON TO KNOW

Press on my mind to know
Press on my heart to glow
Press on my feet to go
Press on my face to show
The wonders of thy love
O Lord
The wonders of thy love

Press on my mind to know
The wonders of thy love

O Lord
The wonders of thy love

Press on my heart to glow
With wonders of thy love
O Lord
With wonders of thy love

Press on my feet to go
Tell wonders of thy love
O Lord
Tell wonders of thy love

Press on my face to show
The wonders of thy love
O Lord
The wonders of thy love

# 188
## FIT 2 PRESS ON AHEAD

Your past is past
Don't dwell on the past
What's past is gone
What's done is done
Dwell not on what's behind you
Think about what's before you

Forgetting what's behind
Press on to what's before
Let Jesus control your mind
He has good things in store
Keep focused on the goal
He will refresh your soul

*Philippians 3:13-14*

## 189
## FIT 2 PRESS ON ALWAYS

Press on to know the Lord
Press on to learn His word
Press on today
Press on always

Press on to walk with God
Press on to talk with God
Press on today
Press on always

Press on the Good News share
Press on and everywhere
Press on today
Press on always

Press on till we get home
Press on till work is done
Press on today
Press on always
Press on press on press on

*Hosea 6:3*

## 190
## FIT 2 PROPHESY

Prophesy (preach, teach) for

Edification - to build up

Exhortation – to lift up

Consolation – to cheer up

Speak to people for their good

*1 Corinthians 14:3*

# 191
# FIT 2 RAIN DOWN

Look down
Rain down
Come down

Look down at us
Rain down on us
Come down with us

Look down at us God our Father
Rain down on us Christ our Savior
Come down with us Holy Spirit

Look down at us God our Father
See the travail of our soul

Rain down us on Christ our Savior
Save us heal us make us whole

Come down with us Holy Spirit
Fill us use us take control

*Isaiah 64:1-4*

# 192
# FIT 2 RECEIVE

God's gift to us His Son
God's gift to us His grace

God's gift to us our time
God's gift to us our place

God's gift to us His joy
God's gift to us His peace
God's gift to us our hope
God's gift to us release

God's gift to us His love
God's gift to us His care
God's gift to us our strength
God's gift to us our prayer

God's gift to us His life
God's gift to us His light
God's gift to us our faith
God's gift to us our sight

*2 Corinthians 9:15*

## 193
## FIT 2 RECEIVE UNEXPECTED STRENGTH

Unexpected strength for
Unexpected trials
 This is
 What
 God gives

Unusual blessing for
Unusual burdens
 This is
 What
 God gives

Unexpected strength

Unusual blessing
Undeserved favor
    This is
    What
    God gives

*Isaiah 41:10*

# 194
# FIT 2 RECONCILE

Ambassadors for Christ have a
Ministry of reconciliation with a
Message of reconciliation
Be ye reconciled to God

O Christ my Lord may I be
A good ambassador for Thee
Fulfilling my ministry
Proclaiming faithfully
The message of reconciliation
For all to hear and see

# 195
# FIT 2 REFLECT

Reflect on the passion
Of the Lord

Remember the crucifixion
Of the Lord

Rejoice in the provision
From the Lord

Relax in your position
In the Lord

Rekindle your compassion
Like the Lord

Renew your dedication
To the Lord

Redouble your proclamation
For the Lord

# 196
# FIT 2 REIGN

It is a faithful saying – 1 Timothy 1:15
Christ Jesus came into the world sinners to save

It is a faithful saying – 1 Timothy 4:8
Godliness is profitable for here and now and there and then

It is a faithful saying – 2 Timothy 2:12
If we suffer with Him with Him we shall also reign

It is a faithful saying – Titus 3:8
As believers we must be careful good works to maintain

The root of salvation – Christ came to save – the cross to bear
The privilege of salvation – eternal life – now here then there
The reward of salvation – the crown of life – a crown to wear
The result of salvation – a faith that works – a faith to share

# 197
# FIT 2 REJOICE

Rejoice give thanks and sing
Give thanks in every thing
Sing halleluiahs to the King
Rejoice give thanks and sing

Rejoice in Christ alone
He sits upon the throne
He died for sinners to atone
Rejoice in Christ alone

Rejoice in Father God
Sing praise and give Him laud
He sent His Spirit from above
Rejoice in Father God

Rejoice He comes again
O'er all the earth to reign
Let men and angels sing amen
Rejoice He comes again

# 198
# FIT 2 REMEMBER AND MEDITATE

I remember the days of old
I think about all of Your deeds
I meditate on the work of Your hands
How You provide all of our needs

I remember the days of old
I think about all of Your care
I meditate on the love of Your heart
How You always answer our prayer

I remember the days of old
I think about all of Your power
I meditate on the strength of Your arms
And the victory hour by hour

*Psalm 143:5*

# 198a
# LIKE A BIRD

### Isaiah 31:5a
*Like birds hovering, so the Lord of hosts will protect Jerusalem*

This picture of God's protection brought to mind the times I have seen birds hovering. They hover for several reasons. When they hover over an area, eagles and hawks are watching what is going on below them. The hawk can see all kinds of activity as he hovers, just as God sees all. Nothing escapes His eye. This is the hovering of watching.

I have watched live video feeds of an eagle at her nest with an eaglet, and her hovering is different but no less diligent. There are times when she seems to be looking around, oblivious to the baby near her feet, yet as soon as the baby moves, her eyes revert immediately to the baby's needs. This is the hovering of provision.

Another picture of hovering is the duck swimming with her 18 ducklings. She is in the lead and all the ducklings are swimming behind her, but not always in a perfect line. They swim here and there, sometimes stopping to investigate something. The mother appears unaware and yet as the ducklings become distracted and begin lagging behind, she turns around and gathers them all back together before they go any further. This is the hovering of leading.

I recently noticed a bird in my back yard, flying from bush to fence and back again all the while making a great deal of noise as a cat walked through the yard. That mother bird was hovering in a totally different way but hovering nonetheless. She was protecting her nest from that cat.

All these birds hovered, each one in a different way and for a different reason. Each hovering bird represents a way in which God hovers over His children: watching us, protecting us, providing for us, and guiding us. *Like birds hovering, so the Lord of hosts will protect Jerusalem.*

# 199
# FIT 2 REMEMBER

Remember His marvelous works
Remember His wonders of old
Remember the words of His mouth
Remember and let it be told

Works so marvelous
Wonders so mighty
Words so meaningful

*Psalm 105:5*

# 200
# FIT 2 REMEMBER GOD'S GRACE

Rocks of Remembrance

Remember to gather up
All the displays
Of God's good grace
Build a grand memorial
Mark how we've come
This far by faith

Praising God in this place

As His good grace we trace
Mile markers of His mercy
Monuments of His grace

## 201
## FIT 2 REMEMBER TO REST

My dear father used to say
And I remembered just today

Come apart for a while
And Rest
Or fall apart after a while
In Ruin

Maybe it was
Come apart for a while
And rest
Or just come all apart

He said the choice was ours
But it always affected other too
So plan to have some special hours
For work and play and rest for you
Keep the balance every day
For work and play and time to pray

And I remembered just today
What my father used to say

## 202
## FIT 2 REMEMBER AND REACH

Remember the cross of Jesus
Reflect on the love of Jesus

Repent at the feet of Jesus

Rejoice in the victory of Jesus
Relax in the presence of Jesus
Rest in the arms of Jesus

Recall the command of Jesus
Repeat the message of Jesus
Reach the world for Jesus

# 203
# FIT 2 RESTORE

Revive us
And we will call upon thy name
Restore us
And we will obey

Revive us
In the midst of the year
Restore us
And we will not fear

Revive us
And we will sing thy praise
Restore us
And we will obey

Revive us
So we can run the race
Restore us
And we'll see thy face

Restore us
And we will be saved
And we will not fear

And we will obey
And we'll see thy face

*Psalm 80:18-19*

# 204
# FIT 2 RETIRE

R Regular routines required no more

E Ending one phase of life
    Entering another with delight

T Treasured memories of
    Triumph in trial

I Incredible illustrations of
    Godly influencing

R Rejoicing in an uncharted future
    With resources from
    An unchanging God

E Encountering more challenges
    With less change
    Enjoying more mess
    With less stress

# 205
# FIT 2 REVEL

Reveling in the glory
Of God's creation
Basking in His great love

My sure foundation
Rejoicing in the joy
Of my salvation
Resting in a heavenly
Contemplation

*Psalm 40:5*

## 206
## FIT 2 RULE FOREVER

You will rule forever Lord
You are King for all time too
Bring us back to you O Lord
Give us a fresh new start with you

*Lamentations 5:19*

## 207
## FIT 2 RULE

God rules the army in heaven above
And earthlings here below
He works His will with a heart of love
His blessing to bestow

God works His pleasure in earth and heaven
And none can stay His hand
His will our treasure let praise be given
And sound through out the land

*Daniel 4:35*

# 208
# FIT 2 RUN WITH PATIENCE

Run with patience the race
With the Spirit keep pace
Lay aside every weight
The sin that easily besets
Finish without regrets
Looking at Jesus' face

*Hebrews 12:1*

# 209
# FIT 2 RUN

Throw off everything that hinders you
Run with perseverance your race
Fix your eyes on Jesus
Consider Him who endured
Then you won't loose heart and quit

Throw it off - (simplify)
Run your race - (persevere)
Fix your eyes - (meditate)
Look to Him - (encouragement)
Do not quit - (obedience)

*Hebrews 12:1-3*

# 210
# FIT 2 SCATTER

Scatter seeds of kindness
Every where you go
Scatter seeds of goodness

Let God make them grow

# 211
# FIT 2 SEEK AND THANK

Give thanks and pray
Make known and sing
Talk ye and praise
Rejoice seek Him

*Psalm 105:1-5*

# 212
# FIT 2 SEEK

You will sin when you set
Not your heart to seek the Lord

Set your heart
    Prepare your mind
    Determine your will
    Focus your life

Seek the Lord
    Want his will
    Obey his word
    Walk his way
    Worship his wonder

Do you set your heart
    Prepare
    Determine and
    Focus you life?

Do you seek the Lord

Want
Obey
Walk his way
Worship his wonder every day?

Walk in his way for there's no other way
To be happy in Jesus but to walk in his way

"He did evil because he prepared
Not his heart to seek the Lord"

*2 Chronicles 12:14*

# 213
# FIT 2 SEEK THE LORD

Ye meek of the earth
Seek ye the Lord
Seek His righteousness
Seek His meekness
Seek His face evermore

*Zephaniah 2:3*

# 214
# FIT 2 SEEK THOSE THINGS

Seek those things
Which are above
Seek His wisdom
And His love

Seek the Lord
He can be found
Seek His grace

Be heaven bound

Seek His likeness
And His life
Seek His meekness
In the strife

Seek His glory
Here below
Seek His love
To others show

Seek His
Righteousness alone
Seek to worship
At His throne

Seek to praise Him
All day long
Seek to thank Him
With your song

*Colossians 3:1*

# 215
# FIT 2 SEEK HIM

Seek and you will find
    (Matthew 7:7)
Seek the Lord while he may be found
    (Isaiah 55:6)
Seek the Lord that you may live
    (Amos 5:4, 6)
Seek the Lord on Holy Ground

# SECTION
## 9

## EAT PROPERLY

"In the night, Lord, I remember your name, that
I may keep your law. This has been my practice."
— Psalm 119:55-56

## 216
## FIT 2 SERVE

To be a servant to the churches
Was Isaac Watts' design
To be a helper
To the joy of every Christian

To exalt himself
To the rank of poet
Was not even is his mind
To get glory
For his hymns not his ambition

To be a servant to the churches
Is Russ D. Rhodes design
To be a helper
To the joy of every Christian

To exalt myself
To the rank of poet
Is not even in my mind
To get glory
For my hymns not my ambition

*Psalm 95:1*

## 216a
## JUST A FLEA

**Isaiah 41:13**

*For I am the Lord you God who takes hold of your right hand
and says to you, Do not fear; I will help you.*

One of the most heartwarming sights we see is a father holding the hand
of a small child as they walk down the street. This is the picture of Isaiah

41:13, a picture of God's love, His father-like care of His children, walking beside them, holding their hand.

He takes hold of my hand and helps me because like a small child I am too weak to walk very far on my own. My ability to walk any distance comes from His taking hold of my spiritual hand. God is adding His strength to mine just as the father's strength keeps the child upright and able to continue walking. I can face anything because my heavenly father is taking hold of my right hand, helping me walk.

This verse reminds me of the story of the flea that crossed the bridge by riding in the elephant's ear. When they reached the other side of the bridge, the flea whispered to the elephant, "My, didn't we shake that bridge?" It is really all God, but with Him holding my right hand, we do it together.

## 217
## FIT 2 SERVE GOD

God is so good
He cares for me
He answers prayer
He's so good to me

I'll walk with God
We'll talk today
I'll walk with God
All along the way

I'll serve the Lord
I'll read His Word
I'll serve the Lord
Every passing day

## 218
## FIT 2 SERVE OTHERS

SERVANTHOOD – serving others
leads to your
SUFFERING – seen by others
leads to the
SALVATION of others

## 219
## FIT 2 SERVE WITH PASSION

Hear His Word
Understand His work
Love His ways
Serve with praise
To God

Hear Him now
Understand and bow
Love His person
Serve with passion
The Lord

*John 8:43*

## 220
## FIT 2 SERVE FAITHFULLY

To serve God is
To follow Christ Jesus
God the Son

To serve God is
To know the presence of

God the Spirit

To serve God is
To enjoy the honor of
God the Father

Lord, may I serve You with
Regular Renewal
Constant Commitment
Daily Devotion and a
Forever Focus

Lord, may I serve You more
Faithfully
Enthusiastically
Consistently and
Joyfully

Lord, may I serve You and
Follow Your footsteps
Know Your presence and
Enjoy Your honor
Amen and Amen

*John 12:26*

## 221
## FIT 2 SHOUT

Shout shout shout about

The Christ child born in Bethlehem
Peace on the earth good will toward men
The shepherds in the field that night
Were startled by the heavenly light
The angels in the sky did sing

The Savior full salvation brings
Glory to the King of Kings

Shout shout shout it out

*Luke 2*

## 222
## FIT 2 SHOW

Show me now thy way
That I may truly know thee
Show me now thy grace
That I may fully know thee
Show me now thy glory
Help me tell the story
Of thy redeeming love
Sent down from heaven above

*Exodus 33:13*

## 223
## FIT 2 SING 4 JOY

S – Satisfying Sovereign Savior
I – Indwelling instructing Holy Spirit
N – New mercies given everyday
G – Grace greater then all our sin

4 winds of praise from
4 corners of the earth
4 all times night and day
4 all they're worth

J – Justified freely through Jesus' blood

O – Obsessed with His overflowing love
Y – Yielding to His will, yearning for His return

They shall sing in the ways of the Lord
They shall bring all their praise to the Lord
The shall sing and rejoice
The shall shout with one voice
They shall sing in the ways of the Lord

*Psalm 138:5*

# 224
# FIT 2 SING

Singing His praise
During the day
Praising the Lord
Recalling His Word

During the night
Without any sight
Remember His name
When you're awake

Serve Him in the morning
Remembering His ways
Thank Him in the evening
Praising all the day

*Psalm 119:54-55*

## 225
# FIT 2 SING HIS SONGS

I sing His songs
Throughout each night
Praying to God
Who gives me life

*Psalm 42:8*

## 226
# FIT 2 SING GLORY

In the mornin' Lord
You're gonna hear my voice
In the mornin' Lord
I will sacrifice
In the mornin' in the mornin' Lord

In the mornin' Lord
I wanna hear Your Word
In the mornin' Lord
I wanna do what I heard
In the mornin' in the mornin' Lord

At the noontime Lord
I will lift my hands
At the noontime Lord
Do as You command
At the noontime at the noontime Lord

In the evenin' Lord
I will stop and pray
In the evenin' Lord
I will praise Your name
In the evenin' in the evenin' Lord

In the evenin' Lord
When I've done my best
In the evenin' Lord
Then it's time to rest
In the evenin' in the evenin' Lord

And at anytime Lord
When I hear Your voice
And at anytime Lord
Then I start to rejoice

And at anytime anytime Lord

And in glory Lord
When I look on Your face
I sing glory Lord
For Your amazing grace
I sing glory I sing glory Lord
I sing glory I sing glory Lord

*Psalm 5:3*

## 227
## FIT 2 SING HIS PRAISE

Jesus holds my hand
He walks with me
He talks with me
Jesus holds my hand

Jesus holds my hand
Jesus guides me on
Jesus hears my cry
Jesus gives a song

Jesus hears my cry
He listens long
He makes me strong
Jesus hears my cry

Jesus cares for me
He hears my prayers
I know he cares
Jesus cares for me

Jesus guides me on
He leads the way
From day to day
Jesus guides me on

Jesus gives a song
To him I sing
My praises bring
Jesus gives a song

Jesus holds my hand
Jesus guides me on
Jesus hears my cry
Jesus gives a song

*Isaiah 41:10, 13*

## 228
## FIT 2 SING ON

Sing on O barren one sing on
God will turn your barrenness to blessing
Sing on O barren one sing on

Sing on O doubting one sing on
God will turn your doubting into shouting
Sing on O doubting one sing on

Sing on O helpless one sing on
God will send you help and hope and healing
Sing on O helpless one sing on

Sing on O believer sing on
This will cheer your heart and bring rejoicing
Sing on O believer sing on

*Isaiah 54:1*

## 229
## FIT 2 SIT WALK STAND

Power in Prayer, Ephesians

SIT – 1:20, 2:6
WALK – 4:1, 17; 5:2, 8, 13
STAND – 6:11, 13-14

*Ephesians 5:14*

## 230
## FIT 2 SOAR HIGH

Lord
My hope is in You
My strength to renew
Then will I
Soar high
Run long
Walk steady
With a song

*Isaiah 40:31*

## 231
## FIT 2 SOW

GOD GIVES

LTL – Life to Love
GTG – Grace to Grow
PTP – Power to Pray
STS – Strength to Sow

## 232
## FIT 2 SPEAK

Speak low my friend speak low
It brings down the highest temper
Speak slow my friend speak slow
It reduces the fastest tongue
Speak little my friend speak little
It keeps you out of much trouble

*James 1:19*

## 233
## FIT 2 STAND

Take my hand dear Father
Help me stand
When the way is long
And I've lost my song
Take my hand dear Father
Help me stand

*Take my hand take my hand*
*Help me stand help my stand*
*Take my hand Dear Father*
*(Dear Jesus, O Spirit)*
*Help me stand*

Take my hand dear Jesus
Help me stand
When the path is steep
And I've lost my peace
Take my hand dear Jesus
Help me stand

Take my hand O Spirit
Help me stand
When the road is rough
And I've had enough
Take my hand O Spirit
Help me stand

## 234
## FIT 2 STAND FIRM

Who may enjoy God's presence?
He who walks uprightly
He who works righteously

He who speaks truthfully
He who treats others fairly
He who keeps his word faithfully
Do this and thus stand firm

*Psalm 15*

# 234a
# WHAT DO YOU REALLY WANT?

### Luke 18:41
*"What do you want me to do for you?" He said,
"Lord, let me recover my sight."*

When Jesus asked the blind beggar what He wanted, the man asked for his sight. He could have asked for a new set of clothes. He was a beggar so I am quite certain he did not have nice clothes. He could have asked for enough money to live on for a while. That way he would not have to beg to get the essentials of life taken care of.

Instead of asking for money or food or clothing, he asked to have his sight recovered. Why? Because he understood that his most basic need was not the clothes he was wearing or the amount of money he had in his pocket. He understood that recovering his sight would bring with it the answer to most, if not all his other needs. That is how God wants me to respond to Him. He wants to provide me with my basic need for salvation and spiritual renewal and in turn I will get everything I need. It is Matthew 11:33 in action: "Seek first the kingdom of God and his righteousness, all these things shall be added unto you."

# 235
# FIT 2 STAND STILL

Stand still and know that:
I am God
    He is God alone
    He is in control

I am Alpha and Omega
    He is all in all
    He is all I need

I am the Way
    He is my guide
    He holds my hand

I am the Truth
    He keeps His word
    He is always near

I am the Life
    He gives me life
    He helps me stand

I am the Resurrection
    He gives me hope
    He is my confidence

I am the Bread of Life
    He feeds my soul
    He makes me whole

I am the Light of the world
    He lights my way
    He plans my day

I am the Door of the sheep
    He is my protection
    He keeps me safe

I am the Good Shepherd
    He cares for me
    He loves me so

I am the True Vine
    He makes me fruitful
    He blesses my life

## 236
## FIT 2 STAND TALL

STAND UP
For the truth absolute
For the absolute truth about God
For right living before men
For right standing before God

STAND OUT
Be good godly and gracious
Be respectful and thankful
Be compassionate and caring
Be kind patient and fruitful

STAND TALL
In the strength of Christ the Lord
In obeying His command and His call
In reading and heeding His word
In helping the weak lest they fall

Stand up
Stand OUT
And to all
STAND TALL

*Ephesians 6:11-15*

## 237
## FIT 2 STAND UP

In the face of Problems
Pain and Persecution

We don't stand down
We face the opposition

We don't stand with the enemy
 We stay with God's people
We don't stand against the foe
 We pray not criticize

We STAND UP for the
 Right things and for the
 Right reasons and get the
 Right results

# 238
# FIT 2 START NOW

Procrastination saps your power
Completion brings relief
DO IT NOW this very hour
And save yourself some grief

# 239
# FIT 2 STAY

Stay close
Stay connected
Remain faithful
Remain fruitful

Stay close to the Christ of the cross
Stay connected to remove all the dross
Remain faithful in deed and in word
Remain fruitful in serving the Lord

Stay close to the Lord of your life
Stay connected through sorrow and strife
Remain faithful in word and in deed
Remain fruitful by sowing the seed

*John 15:4* The branch
cannot bear fruit of itself

## 240
## FIT 2 STAY CLOSE

Turn away from God
And He will
Turn away from you

Look for Him
And you will
Surely find Him

Stay with God
And he will
Stay with you

Turn toward God
Look for God
Stay close to God

*2 Chronicles 15:2*

## 241
## FIT 2 SUBMIT

Submission to God's sovereignty is
Believing without comprehending
Obeying without understanding
Going without knowing

*Genesis 12*
*Hebrews 11:8*

## 242
## FIT 2 SUBMIT AFTER GOD

Long after the LORD
Groan after GOD
Seek after the SAVIOR
Follow after the FATHER
Search after the SON
Submit to the SPIRIT
Call out to CHRIST
Rejoice in JESUS

*Romans 8:23*

## 243
## FIT 2 TAKE

Take the low road
Of humble sacrificial service
Take the deep valley
Of valuable time in the shadows
Take the bitter pill
Of personal pain and suffering
Take the little lane
That sometimes leads to loneliness
Take up the daily cross
Of Christ and His loving correction
Take all things from
God's bleeding heart and tender hands
Take up your harp
And sing His praise throughout the land

LORD help me take
The low road The deep valley
The bitter pill The little lane
The daily cross Yea all things

In Your gracious will
Singing praises still

## 244
## FIT 2 TALK

The walk of the feet
The strength of the arms
The bend of the knee
The cry of the heart

The thought of the mind
The sigh of the soul
The light of the eye
In Jesus control

The bent of the back
The stress and the strain
The bow of the head
Again and again

The talk of the tongue
The work of the hands
The song and the voice
At Jesus command

## 245
## FIT 2 TEACH

Prepare your heart for God
Seek the Law of God
Do the will of God
    Then
Teach the Word of God

*Ezra 7:10*

## 246
## FIT 2 THANK THE LORD

Thank You Lord
For full salvation through the blood
of Calvary's death
For godly parents who lived
and walked a life of faith
For every burden that keeps me
on my knees Your will to please
For every trial that makes me
stronger with patience longer
For prayers You've answered
and those You chose to say no
For joy and sorrow – You have
a plan and purpose for each one
Yes LORD my heart is bursting with thanks
and praise for who You are and what You say
and how You bless me every day

## 247
## FIT 2 THINK

Think about His love
Think about His mercy
Think about His grace
Think about His faithfulness and power

Show the world His love
Show the world His kindness
Let them see His face
Let them see His faithfulness each hour

God is good God is kind
God is faithful all the time
God is close God is near
God is present God is here

# 248
# FIT 2 TRAVEL

Order my steps in thy word
Keep me walking day by day
In sweet fellowship
With thee Lord
Travelling on the narrow way
Step by step hour by hour
May each moment
Know thy power.

*Psalm 119:133*

# 249
# FIT 2 TRUST

His loving eyes are always upon you
His helping hands are there to lead you
His caring heart is always thinking of you

Rest in His great love
Hold His strong hand
Trust His big heart

# 250
# FIT 2 TRUST THE LORD

Trust the Lord

He is merciful
He is faithful
He is powerful
Trust the Lord
He will forgive you
He will save you
He will hear you
He will help you
Trust you must
Trust trust
The Lord

*Psalm 130 & 131*

## 251
## FIT 2 TRUST IN THE LORD

It is better to trust in the Lord
Than to put confidence in man
It is better to trust in the Lord
And watch Him unfold His good plan

It is better to trust in the Lord
Than to put confidence in princes
It is better to trust in the Lord
Who always keep His promises

Trust in the Lord
Stand tall for God
Hold forth the word
Do what is good

*Psalm 118:8-9*

# SECTION
## *10*

### GET ADEQUATE REST

"Peace I leave with you; my peace I give you. I do not give to you as the world gives. Do not let your hearts be troubled and do not be afraid." — John 14:27

# 252
# FIT 2 TRY

Why me Lord
Why me?
Is what we often say
Try me Lord
Try me
Try me Lord today
And find in me
A hope
That hangs on
With faith
Alone in Thee

# 252a
# BEYOND EXPLANATION

### John 14:27b
*Peace not as the world gives do I give to you.*

How does the world give us peace? How different is it from the peace Jesus gives?

The peace of the world must be earned by work. People are constantly working to find peace in what they do or who they are. They pursue work and wealth, hoping to gain peace in some way from it. Or they try to find peace in pleasure of some kind, whether it be activity or pleasure of some kind or vices such as alcohol or drugs.

There are many instances in history when leaders of nations have held peace talks, looking for ways to obtain peace. However successful treaties are between nations or warring parties, the resulting peace is tenuous at best, and often not successful at all in the end.

The peace that Jesus promised is not the world's kind of peace. It can only be obtained through our faith in Him. We do not work to get it; it is *given* to us. God's gift of peace "passes all understanding" (Philippians 4:7). We get that unexplainable peace only from God and it defies explanation. It can only be explained with experience. It is not peace as the world gives peace.

## 253
## FIT 2 TUNE IN

Tune in each day
To God's channels of grace
Come near and hear
All ye that fear
Our God

Tune in each day
To God's quiet place
Be still and know
God loves you so
For good

Tune in each day
To God's channels of grace
Tune in each day
To God's quiet place

*Psalm 66:16*

## 254
## FIT 2 TURN

Turn us – v.4
   We repent
    God responds
Revive us – v.6

We respond
We rejoice
Show us – v.7
We look
We learn
Grant us – v.7
God gives
We receive
We hear his voice – v.8
God speaks peace
We walk straight
We stay steady
We move forward
In his steps

*Psalm 85:4-13*

# 255
# FIT 2 TURN US

Turn us – back toward God
Face to Face
Revive us – to rejoice in God
Heart to Heart
Show us – the mercy of God
Eye to Eye
Grant us – the deliverance of God
Hand in Hand

*Psalm 85*

## 256
# FIT 2 UNDERSTAND

God understands
When you feel all done in
When you've lost sight of Him
God understands
He understands

*God understands your sorrow*
*God sees each falling tear*
*God plans all your tomorrows*
*God's voice is near to cheer*

God understands
When the road gets so rough
When you've just had enough
God understands
He understands

God understands
When the path isn't clear
When He doesn't seem near
God understands
He understands

God understands
When beset with much care
With trouble every where
God understands
He understands

*God understands your sorrow*
*God sees each falling tear*
*God plans all your tomorrows*
*God's voice is near to cheer*

## 257
## FIT 2 USE

Lord you made me
Renew me
I am your work
Complete me
I am your harp
Please tune me
I am your child
Do teach me
I am just yours
Now use me

*Psalm 119:73*

## 258
## FIT 2 WAIT 4 THE LORD

Your Walk with the Lord
    Keep in step with the Spirit
You Wait for the Lord
    Keep looking for Him to work
Your Word for the Lord
    Keep telling forth His story

## 259
## FIT 2 WAIT

Wait for the Lord
He helps and shields us
Rejoice in the Lord
Trust in His holy name
Hope in the Lord
He shows us His mercy

*Psalm 33:20-22*

## 260
## FIT 2 WAIT AND WATCH

Wait on the Lord
Watch for His return
Wait in His Word
Watch and you will learn

Wait patiently
Watch expectantly
Work and watch and pray
Christ may come today

*Matthew 24:42*

## 261
## FIT 2 WAKE UP

Wake up
Get up and get going for God
Shape up
Be more like Christ in deed and word
Dress up
Put on the full spiritual armor of God
Take up
Take up your cross daily and follow the Lord

## 262
## FIT 2 WALK

Holy Walkers are
Perfect in intensions

Imperfect in attainment

Holy Walkers
Seek God whole heartedly
Keep His testimonies
Praise God uprightly
Walk in all His ways

Holy Walkers
Learn His Holy Word
Joy in His holy name
Preach His mighty work
Meditate again

*Psalm 119:1-16*

## 263
## FIT 2 WALK IN ALL HIS WAYS

What doth the Lord thy God
    Require of thee but

To fear the Lord thy God
To walk in all his ways
To love him
To serve the Lord thy God
    With all thy heart
    With all thy soul

To fear
To walk
To love
To serve with heart and soul

To hear from heaven above
To walk with God in love

To share the gospel story
To give Him all the glory

*Deuteronomy 10:12*

## 264
## FIT 2 WALK AS HE WALKED

Be ready to minister
Be servant of all
Be doing good
Bear one another's burden
Esteem others better than
Be kind one to another
Forgive one another
Walk as He walked

Christ suffered for us…
Follow His steps.

*1 Peter 2:21*

## 265
## FIT 2 WALK BY FAITH

Walking by sight
And not by faith
Fighting your fight
Brings early death

Walking by faith
And not by sight
Do what He says
Bring God delight

*2 Corinthians 5:7*
*Hebrews 11:6*
*Galatians 3:11*
*Romans 14:23*

## 266
## FIT 2 WATCH

Your loins girded
Your lights burning
Like men waiting
God comes knocking
Finds you watching

*Luke 12:35-37*

## 267
## FIT 2 WATCH AND PRAY

Take ye heed and watch and pray
Ye know not when the hour or day
Unto you and unto all I say
Watch watch and pray

Watch and pray every day
Serve the Lord all the way
Watch watch and pray

How near the coming of the Lord
The judge is standing at the door
The things we have shall be no more
Watch watch and pray

The end of all things is at hand
Soon we shall see the Promised Land

Let us be bold and take our stand
Watch watch and pray

*Mark 13:37*


# 268
# FIT 2 WEAR

The threads you weave
In the tapestry of your life
Here below
You will wear
In the robe of rewards
Up above

The threads you weave
Down here
Is what you wear
Up there


# 269
# FIT 2 WEED

Pull from your heart
The good garden of God's grace

Weeds of worry
Roots of bitterness
Thistles of thoughtlessness
Seeds of cynicism and sin

Briers of unbelief
Rocks of rebellion
Thorns of prayerlessness
Stones of stubbornness deep within

# 270
# FIT 2 WIN
# (15 STEPS)

Do the right thing right now
Leave the results with God
Give all the glory to God
Have a thankful heart
Pray in faith believing

Share and care for others
Love and learn God's Word
Fear not man but God only
Forgive and be forgiven
Leave a trail of truth

Prepare down here for up there
Practice the presence of God
Launch out when God says go
Fight the good fight of faith
Run the race to win

# 270a
# KEEP LEARNING

### John 16:12-13
*I still have many things to say to you, but you cannot bear them now. When the Spirit of truth comes, he will guide you into all the truth.*

Learning is a progressive activity. We experience that in our education as children and young adults. Before I could learn to write words, I had to learn the alphabet. I remember well those wide-lined pages on which I practiced making letters the proper way. Later on, before I could study algebra, I had to learn simple mathematics; before physics, I studied general science. The principle remained the same no matter what the subject matter was.

In John 16:12-13, Jesus was applying that same principle. The disciples, even after three years of concentrated learning and experience, could not learn everything there was to know about following Jesus. It would take time. The Holy Spirit, the Spirit of Truth, would be their teacher. In spiritual things, learning is the same as in any area of learning. Before the deep things of God, it is the basics of salvation and forgiveness. I will continue to learn as the Holy Spirit guides my learning program, just as He guided the disciples in the New Testament.

# 271
## FIT 2 WIN AND NOT GIVE IN

God created you to win
So don't give in
Stay close to him
Through thick and thin
Take it on the chin
It's time to begin
And walk away from sin

*Psalm 56:12-13*

# 272
## FIT 2 WIN GOD'S GIFTS

My life my lips are His
My heart my home
My talents and tongue
The stow-able stuff enough
Money and how to make it
Abilities and disabilities
My treasure and pleasure
My time is not mine
My joy and rejoicing
Peace and perseverance

Contentment and calmness
My going and coming
My family and friends
My watching and waiting

All these and more are
Gifts of God's goodness
Cherish them still
Or lose them you will


## 273
## FIT 2 WIN GRACIOUSLY

Go forward fearlessly
Stand strong triumphantly
Fight hard victoriously
Pray much expectantly
Run the race faithfully
Win the prize graciously

*Genesis 46:3-4*


## 274
## FIT 2 WIN BY PRESSING ON

Forgetting behind
Straining before
Putting behind the past
Straining for what will last

Forgetting gone Pressing on
Forgetting gone Pressing on

This one thing I do
Forgetting what is behind

Straining for what's ahead
I press toward the goal
To win the great prize
Toward heavenly skies
In the Lord Jesus Christ

Forgetting gone Pressing on
Forgetting gone Pressing on

*Philippians 3:13*

# 275
# FIT 2 WORK

A mind to work
A heart to pray
Our eyes to watch
Both night and day

Give me a mind to work
O Lord
Give me a heart to pray
Give me eyes to watch
O Lord
And serve You night and day

*Nehemiah 4:6ff*

# 276
# FIT 2 WORK WATCH AND PRAY

It is time for You
O Lord to work
Yes it is time
It is time

It is time for us
To get out of the way
And let You work
Let You work

It is time for us
To watch and pray
O watch and pray
Watch and pray

*Psalm 119:126*

## 277
# FIT 2 WORK WALK AND TALK

My hands to work
My feet to walk
My eyes to see
My mouth to talk

My arms to hold
My brother or sister
Out in the cold
My soul to worship
My heart to praise
My ears to hear

My mind to think
My voice to sing
With thanks to bring
My strength to give
To Christ my Lord
For Him to live

# SECTION
## *11*

## BE DEDICATED TO IMPROVEMENT

"I trust in you, Lord. I say, 'You are my God.' My times are in your hands; deliver me from the hands of my enemies." — Psalm 31:14-15

# 279
# FIT 2 WORSHIP

GOD is Awesome and is
All knowing and all caring
Always here always there
Always ready to answer
All our petitions and prayers

All righteousness all loving-kindness
All holiness all glorious
All magnificent all beneficent
All powerful all merciful all prayerful
Always gentle and tender too
Always doing what is best for you

Always just and
Always just on time
Always ready to help always
Always worthy of all our praise

# 280
# FIT 2 WORSHIP HIM

The Lord reigns
The Lord is great
The Lord is holy
The Lord listens
The Lord answers
The Lord forgives
The Lord is just
The Lord is righteous

Fear Him
Praise Him
Worship Him

Obey Him
Exalt Him
Worship Him

*Psalm 99*

## 281
## FIT 2 WORSHIP THE BABE

Remember the
Babe of Bethlehem is the
Christ of Christmas and the
Coming King of Kings

Oh come let us adore Him
    And
Love Him deeply
Enjoy Him fully
Serve Him faithfully

## 282
## FIT 2 WORSHIP IN TRUTH

Acknowledge God for
Who He really is in truth
Infinitely holy
Infinitely perfect

Infinitely worthy of our
Infinite praise
Infinitely removed
From sin always

Infinitely good with
Infinite love

Infinite kindness with
Grace from above

Infinitely just with
Infinite power
Infinitely present
Hour by hour

Infinite liberty
Infinite light
Infinite Lord with
Infinite might

Infinite knowledge and
Infinite wisdom
Infinite care for
Those in His Kingdom

## 283
## A GOOD MAN

A
Good man is
Gracious and
Generous and will
Guide and
Guard
His talk
His ways
His walk

*Psalm 112:5*

## 284
## AIN'T IT M0MMA?

Cry to Jesus
He cares when I fall down
And hurt myself on the ground

Walk with Jesus
He lifts me with His strong hand
As I get up and try to stand
Ain't it momma?

Sing to Jesus
He loves to hear my voice
When I sing out and rejoice

Dance for Jesus
He looks at me with great delight
When I dance in His presence with all my might
Ain't it momma?

Bow to Jesus
He longs for me to worship Him with praise
And thanksgiving all my days

Fly to Jesus
He takes me in his arms and holds me tight
I'm finally home with Him tonight
Ain't it momma?

## 285
## BE STRONG

Tribute to my faithful father

O father dear

If you were here
O man of flaws and faith
I would recall
The best of all
You served God well 'till death

May I like you
Serve others too
And show the love of God
I would be strong
My whole life long
To walk the path you trod

# 286
# BUILDING BLOCKS FOR THE NEW YEAR

**FAITH:** the foundation stone, Hebrews 11:1-6ff
Joyful confident expectation of eternal salvation
　　The mortar: With all diligence (v.5 and 10)
**MORAL EXCELLENCE:** virtue, 2I Peter 1:3
The right thing
**KNOWLEDGE,** Proverbs 1:7
Knowing the right thing to do
**SELF CONTROL,** Acts 24:25
Only doing the right thing
**PERSEVERANCE,** Luke 21:19
Always doing the right thing
**GODLINESS,** Galatians 5:22-23
Doing the godly thing
**BROTHERLY KINDNESS,** Romans 12:10
Doing the kind thing
**LOVE,** Galatians 5:13-14; Romans 12:9-10
Doing the loving thing
　　More mortar: Be all the more diligent (v.10)

*2 Peter 1:5-10*

# 287
## LIFT UP THE SAINTS OF GOD

Lift up the saints of God
There's someone who needs your prayer
Someone who seems to feel afraid
Someone who needs your care
Remember them in prayer today
And help their burdens to bear
You'll be happy you stopped to pray
For one another

Build up the saints of God
That's something you need to do
Something to help the church of God
Something just right for you
Remember Jesus came to serve
So why not serve Him anew
You'll be happy you're building His church
That lasts forever

# 288
## COMBINING AND CONFUSING

The combining and confusing of contrasts
In opposites and absolutes causes
Consternation, confrontation and chaos

Hot or cold – lukewarm and Useless
Salt or pepper – sand and Worthless
Powerful or weak – Powerless

Good or evil – Wickedness
Wickedness or righteousness – Lawlessness
Do or don't do – sitting Lifeless

Move or don't move - Weakness
Right or wrong – Meaningless
Live 4 God or live 4 self – Purposeless

*Judges 17:6* All the people did whatever seemed right
in their own eyes.

# 289
# CONTINUALLY

*I am continually with thee.*

Continually with God
Continually upon His mind
Continually for my good
Continually before His eyes
    Open wide
Continually in His hand
    Helping me to stand
Continually on His heart
    From the very start
Continually in His favor
Continually in His presence
Continually in His comfort and care
Continually in His peace everywhere

*Psalm 73:23*

# 289a
# THEY ALSO SERVED

### Acts 6:5
*And they chose Stephen, a man full of faith and of the Holy Spirit, and Phillip,
and Prochorus, and Nicanor, and Timon, and Parmenas, and Nicolaus, a
proselyte of Antioch.*

These men also served. We know nothing of them except their names listed here, but Phillip, Prochorus, Nicanor, Timon, Parmenas and Nicolaus all served as the first deacons of the new church that formed following the death and resurrection of Jesus. They were chosen just as Stephen was chosen to serve the needs of the new believers and thus free the apostles for teaching and leading. We know only that they were chosen to serve; they must have done the job because we read about their activities with the believing widows and other needy believers throughout the early chapters of the book of Acts.

They performed their duties under great duress and stress. Their leader Stephen had been arrested and put to death for no other reason than that he was representing Jesus. They had lost their leader and had to face the same opposition Stephen had faced, but it appears that they served in spite of the sadness they felt over his death. They served in spite of the fear that the continuing opposition and danger they faced no doubt caused. *They served* because God's call for them to serve took precedence over any reason to hesitate.

When my time on earth is ended, what will be said about me? That I *also served* in spite of difficulties, in spite of opposition, in spite of discouragements?

# 290
# GOD'S GREAT CREATION

SILENT SECTION
Stars twinkling
Moon glowing
Sun shining
Wind blowing
Clouds moving
Flowers bowing
Butterflies flirting
Branches waving
Trees swaying

Rain falling
Water flowing

SOFT SOUND SECTION
Leaves rustling
Acorns falling
Pine needles whistling
Little branches rubbing

BIG SOUND SECTION

Lightning striking
Clouds clapping
Thunder rolling
Rain beating

STRING SECTION
Crickets strumming
Bees buzzing
Flies flying
Mosquitoes searching
Humming birds humming
Katydid
And others didn't

PERCUSSION SECTION
Woodpeckers pecking
Nuthatches cracking
Squirrels squeaking
Dogs barking
Crows cawing
Geese honking

BASS AND TENOR SECTION
Bull frogs blowing
Tree frogs trolling
Green frogs croaking
Tenor toads
High and low
By the loads

SOPRANO AND
ALTO SECTION
Chickadees screeching
Pine warblers warbling
Cardinals learning
Mockingbirds mocking
Catbirds calling
Robins joining in
Jays just wanting out

SECTION LEADERS
Cats fuss and fight
Over who gets to lead
Most do their best
In the middle of the night
When no one is listening
Others rather be sleeping
When not stalking walking
Begging whining or dinning

This is what we see and hear
Throughout the year
And it's all done
To bring glory to
God's Only Son

*Psalm 8*
*Psalm 33:1-9*
*Psalm 150*

# 291
# DAN DAN THE MUSICAL MAN

Dan Dan the musical man
If you can't play it
He probably can
He plays a pretty good piano
A delightful sounding dulcimer
A terrifically tough trumpet
A piercing penny whistle
And several great guitars
With jazzy Brubeck and
Bach again

With more than a two octave
Vocal range he sang an awesome
Tenor solo in The Messiah
Sings all the parts in the choir
And does a superb performance
Of Comin' Round the Mountain
And the Belly Button Song

He arranges music and writes
And sings very special songs
One for our 25th Anniversary
And another for Thanksgiving
Dan always writes a new song
On his annual winter vacation

Some folks get old and grey and bald
He only has to get old
But he never will
He just keeps on working away
Like the Energizer Bunny everyday
So my young friend
Keep on keeping on
The road well trod
Bringing Glory to

The Son of God

# 292
## DELIVER ME

O God
Deliver me
Hear me
Defend me
Save me
Lead me
Guide me
Pull me

God is
My strong rock
My fortress
My strength
My Redeemer
My Lord

O God
I commit my self
I hate liars
I trust in the Lord
I will be glad and rejoice

*Psalm 31:1-8*

# 293
## EASTER MORNING SONG

You live you live my Savior
You died but live again
You live you live my Savior

You rose up from the grave

My love my love my Savior
My love is what I give
My love my love my Savior
You died that I may live

Your praise your praise my Savior
Your praise is what I bring
Your praise your praise my Savior
Your praise now I will sing

Your will your will my Savior
Your will O may I do
Your will your will my Savior
To serve and worship you

# 294
# EASTER SONG

The cross the cross my Savior
The rugged cross of shame
The cross the cross my Savior
T'was there you took my blame

Your love your love my Savior
Your love how could it be?
Your love your love my Savior
That you would die for me

My sin my sin my Savior
You bore my sin that day
My sin my sin my Savior
You washed it all away

Your life your life my Savior

Your life you freely gave
Your life your life my Savior
My wounded soul to save

## 295
## ENLARGE

Jabez prayed
Enlarge my coast
God granted his request

Solomon asked for wisdom
God gave him what is best
Largeness of heart

When we ask God
For more territory
God gives us time to trust

When we ask God
For more opportunity
God gives us openness to His will

When we ask God
For broader ministry
God gives us a bigger heart

Stretch my heart
In every part
Grant me Lord
A fresh new start

*1 Chronicles 4:10*
*1 Kings 4:29*
*Psalm 91:15*

# 296
# FIT 2 B FREE

God has a plan for man.
He set us free to be
Men who:

Live righteously
Serve faithfully
Pray expectantly

Walk consistently
Run cautiously
Try repeatedly
Fight victoriously

Worship heartily
Praise thankfully
Bless abundantly
Sing joyfully

Work tirelessly
Watch carefully
Wait patiently
Look hopefully

Dig deeply
Sow creatively
Reap abundantly

Read broadly
Think critically
Know confidently
Preach powerfully

Bow humbly
Speak softly
Love godly

Give generously
Share unselfishly
Grow continuously

Learn eagerly
Listen quietly
Die graciously

*John 8:32, 36* And ye shall know
the truth,
And the truth shall make you free.
If the Son shall make you free,
Ye shall be free indeed.

# SECTION
## *12*

## WORK TO IMPROVE
## YOUR SKILL LEVEL

"All Scripture is God-breathed and is useful for teaching, rebuking, correcting and training in righteousness, so that the servant of God may be thoroughly equipped for every good work."
— 2 Timothy 3:16-17

# 297
## FIT 2 BECOME HOLY

We worship God for
Who He is
What He says
What He does

We worship God for
He always does
Just what He says
Because of who He is

He is separate
He is infinite
He is immaculate
He is HOLY

He is personal
He is powerful
He is faithful
He is LOVE

He communicates
He regenerates
He keeps His word
He grants us grace

His holiness we do receive
When we at first believe
What he works in
We can work out
Becoming more like Him

This task on earth
Is never done
Till we arrive at

Heaven and home

## 298
## FIT 2 B IN THE WORD

In the WORD of God:
I can SEE the face of God
I can HEAR the voice of God
I can LEARN the ways of God
I can DISCOVER the will of God

I can OBSERVE the works of God
I can EXPERIENCE the love of God
I can ACCEPT the forgiveness of God
I can KNOW the peace of God
I can SING in praise to God

I can OBEY the word of God
I can ENJOY the presence of God
I can SERVE with the power of God
I can GROW in confidence toward God
I can CHANGE to become more like God

Give me a strong desire O LORD
To be more and more in your WORD

*2 Timothy 3:16-17*

## 299
## FIT 2 B IN TOUCH

In touch
With God and His word
For faith in need

In tune
With the Spirit and His way
To intercede

In time
To listen and learn to obey
And follow His lead

# 300
# FIT 2 B LINKED

Linked to the Father
Linked to the Son
Linked to the Spirit
Linked Three in One

Linked to the Lord
Linked to his peace
Linked to his Word
Linked to increase

Linked to each other
Linked in the fight
Linked to a brother
Linked day and night

# 301
# FIT 2 B OR NOT 2 B

Be joyful in hope
Be patient in tribulation
Be constant in prayer

Be thankful in everything
Be grateful without hesitation

Be thoughtful and care

Be gentle with others
Be calm in frustration
Be quiet and hear

Be serving a brother
Be living without reservation
Be willing to share

*Romans 12:12*

## 302
## FIT 2 B READY

Lord help me B in the
Right place at the
Right time for the
Right reasons with
Right results

Lord help me B
Ready 2 go
Ready 2 stay
Ready 2 wait
Ready 2 pray

Lord help me B
Ready 2 work
Ready 2 rest
Ready 2 always
Give God my best

*Romans 11:33*

## 303
## FIT 2 B SINGING

Singing I go along life's road
For Jesus is with me I know
He's with me where ever I go
His blessing on me doth bestow
His likeness He wants me to show

Singing I go when climbing the hill
Singing I go along life's road
Singing I go and singing still
For Jesus has lifted my load

Singing I go along life's way
For Jesus is with me today
He guideth me day after day
Holding my hand lest I stray
Hearing my cry as I pray

Singing I go when climbing the hill
Singing I go along life's road
Singing I go and singing still
For Jesus has lifted my load

*Psalm 108:1-3*
*Psalm 33:1-4*

## 304
## FIT 2 B STRONG AND COURAGEOUS

Be strong be strong
And let your heart
Take courage
All you
Who

Hope in the Lord

Trust in the Lord
Obey his command
Follow his word
Hold his big hand

Be strong be strong
And let your heart
Take courage
All you
Who
Wait for the Lord

Wait for the Lord
Be patient and true
Follow his steps
He will guide you thru

Be strong be strong
And let your heart
Take courage
All you
Who
Wait for the Lord

*Psalm 31:24*

## 305
## FIT 2 B THANKING

Babies eat
Children play
Teens sometimes wander astray
Fathers work
Mothers pray

Seniors worry their time away

Praising God
Thanking him
We don't do it
That's a sin

## 306
## FIT 2 B TIED

SAMSON
He was promised
    To his mother by God
He was given
    Special power from God
He was early on
    Disobedient to God
He was even so
    Used by God
He was tricked
    To wander from God

SAMSON
He was a Judge
    Of Judah for God
He was clever with
    The wisdom from God
He was punished
    By the enemies of God
He was repentant
    For his sin against God
He was used
    One last time by God

SAMSON
He was very strong physically

He was strong willed mentally
He was not very strong spiritually

God is always faithful
Even when we are not

*Judges 15 and 16*
*Psalm 103:10-11*

## 307
## FIT 2 BRING

God brought all them
Into the land of Ham

He increased his people
He made them strong
He sent them Moses
Bringing Aaron along

He showed his wonders
He sent darkness too
He slew their fish
Now what could they do
He spoke the word
Then came frogs flies lice

He gave them hail-stones
Along with the rain
And smote their land
With fires of flame

God smote their vines
Destroyed the trees
With his power divine
Did just as he pleased

He spoke the word then
Came grass-hoppers
And caterpillars
To plague the land

He smote the first-born
Of all creatures and men
And how they did mourn
Again and again

He brought them forth
With much silver and gold
And strength to be bold
He spread a cloud
And a pillar of fire
He gave them all
Their heart's desire

He opened the rock
And waters flowed out
He carried them through
The desert years

WHY ALL THIS CARE?

God remembered his
Promise to Abraham
He would bring them into
The Promised Land

He brought forth his people
With joy and gladness
He gave lands of the heathen
Now full of sadness

WHY THIS LOVE?

That they might
Keep His statutes
And observe His laws

SUMMING IT UP

He moved them in
He built them up

He brought them out
He carried them through
He brought them back

He wants their praise
Their desire to obey
All of their days

*Psalm 105*

## 307a
## YOU LIFT UP MY HEAD

### Psalm 3:3
*But you are a shield around me, O Lord; you bestow glory
on me and lift up my head.*

How do you know when you are seeing someone sad or discouraged? Discouragement, sadness and defeat are all pictured the same way, as one whose head is bowed down, shoulders slumped forward, eyes closed. Without speaking a single word you know automatically that person is discouraged and disheartened.

The word picture in this verse from Psalm three gives us the picture of what God does for us when we find ourselves in the middle of difficult or uncertain circumstances. The author of this psalm says that God is around him, shielding him. Knowing that God is protecting me builds up my confidence and gives me strength and courage to face difficulties and challenges in a way I could not do on my own.

God lifts up my head, a sign of courage and a positive outlook. I look up instead of down. His presence gives me encouragement. Knowing He is protecting and guiding me means I do not need to feel ashamed of my situation or worried about it. It gives me reason to lift up my head.

## 308
## FIT 2 DELIVER THEM

Our fathers trusted
God delivered them
Our fathers obeyed
God blessed them

Our fathers rebelled
God punished them
Our fathers reacted
God rebuked them

Our fathers repented
God restored them
Our fathers hungered
God feed them

Our fathers grumbled
God troubled them
Our fathers complained
God sustained them

Our fathers wandered
God lead them
Our fathers trusted
God delivered them

*Psalm 22:4*

## 309
## FIT 2 GIVE

Give up
Give in
Give up to God
And not to sin

Give some
Give all
Give all to God
It came from Him

Give soon
Give now
Give now to God
You're sure to win

Give up to God
Give all give now
Give what He gives
Give back to Him

*Deuteronomy 30:14-15*

## 310
## FIT 2 GIVE GENEROUSLY

Give my friend give again
Give generously and then
You will receive the more
With good measure
Heaped up and
Pressed down and
Running over
Help a brother

Help one another
Be a blessing
And be doubly blessed

*Proverbs 11:25*

## 311
## FIT 2 GO AHEAD

God is God alone
God is the
Go-ahead God
God is the
Go-behind God
God is the
Go-with us God

*Deuteronomy 31:8*

## 312
## FIT 2 KEEP

Keep your mouth and
Keep your tongue will
Keep you out of trouble

Keep your hands and
Keep your feet will
Keep you from a stumble

Keep your eyes and
Keep your focus will
Keep you from a fumble

Keep your mind and
Keep your heart will
Keep you from a grumble

*Proverbs 21:23*

## 313
## FIT 2 KEEP ON

Keep on a listenin'
Keep on a witnessin'
Keep on keepin' on keepin

Keep on a talkin' talkin'
Keep on a walkin' walkin'
Keep on keepin' on keepin'

Keep on a prayin' prayin'
Keep on a stayin' stayin'
Keep on keepin' on keepin'

Keep on a fightin' fightin'
Keep on a writin' writin'
Keep on keepin' on keepin"

## 314
## FIT 2 KNOW GOD'S POWER

Doing a little less
Enjoying it a lot more

Getting to know myself

Getting to know my family

Getting to know my good friends

Getting to know God my best FRIEND

Getting to know what matters most

Getting time to read and meditate

Getting time to practice and sing

Getting time to think and pray

Getting time to write a poem
nearly every day

That I may know Him
and the power of
His resurrection

*Philippians 3:10*

# 315
# FIT 2 LIFT UP

I will lift up my hands
    To praise the Lord
I will lift up my voice
    His praise to sing
I will lift up my eyes
    Unto His Word
I will lift up thanksgiving
    Now to bring

I will lift up a brother
    Deep in sin
I will lift another

Full of need
I will lift up a neighbor
    God could win
I will lift up them all
    And intercede

I will lift up a hand
    My help to give
I will lift up my heart
    My love to show
I will lift up a prayer
    That they might live

I will lift up my feet
   And forward go

I will lift up my eyes
   Unto the hill
I will lift up my mind
   And wait alone

I will bow down in silence
   And be still
I will worship my God
   Upon His throne

*Psalm 121*

## 316
## FIT 2 PLAN

Plan before you take a step
Stand before you start to walk
Look where you're going
Go where you're looking
Think before you start to talk
And always ask yourself
Is it true?
Is it necessary?
Is it really helpful?
Plan to listen between the lines
Plan to listen more and talk less
Plan to make the most of your time
Plan to always do what is best

## 317
## FIT 2 PRESS ON TO BRING THE WORD

Press on the know the Lord
Press on to know His Word
Press on to know His world

Press on to bring
The word
Of the Lord

To the world

*Hosea 6:3*

## 318
## FIT 2 REMEMBER MORE

REMEMBER my song
My midnight musings
And meditations

REMEMBER the years
Of God's faithfulness
Goodness and grace

REMEMBER His works
To guide by our side
Ahead and behind

REMEMBER His wonders
Miracles and the touch
Of his helping hands

REMEMBER His ways
Holy and great
Declaring His power
Delivering His people

REMEMBER His people
Who went before us clearing
The path and cheering us on
To heaven at last

*Psalm 77:1, 10-11*
*Hebrews 12:1*

# 319
# FIT 2 REMEMBER AND THANK

Give God thanks
Call upon His name
Make Him known
His great love proclaim

Seek the Lord
Seek His strength
Seek His face evermore

Remember His works
Remember His wonders
Remember His words of yore

Give God thanks
Call upon His name
Make Him known
His great love proclaim

*Psalm 105:1, 4-5*

# 320
# FIT 2 SHAKE

Oh God

SHAKE DOWN
Our indifference
Passive religiosity
Self-satisfaction and
Selfish pleasure

BREAK DOWN
Our reckless living

And Rebellious
Resistance as
Recalcitrant reprobates

TAKE DOWN
Our walls of isolation
Hibernation frustration
Stagnation separation
And hesitation

COME DOWN
To rekindle renew
Restore and rebuild us
Our families and
Our nation

Amen and amen

# 321
# FIT 2 SING AND SERVE

In the shadow of his wing
In his presence I will sing
With my offering I will bring
Praises to my glorious King

May I learn to do His will
When I'm climbing up the hill
Or when stopping to be still
May his Spirit with me fill

Help me Lord quick to obey
Always do just what you say
Never argue or delay
Serving others every day

*Psalm 91:1*

## 322
## FIT 2 SING A SONG

Sing a song of love
Sing a song with joyful chorus
Sing a song for God is with us
Sing a song of love

Sing a song of joy
Sing a song with grateful pleasure
Sing a song of heavenly treasure
Sing a song of joy

Sing a song to God the Father
Sing a song to Christ the Son
Song a song to the Holy Spirit
Song a song to the Three-in-One

Sing a song of praise
Sing a song our God has given
Sing a song our home is heaven
Sing a song of praise

Sing a song of thanks
Sing a song O my dear brother
Sing a song give thanks together
Sing a song of thanks

Sing a song of love
Sing a song of praise
Sing a song of thanks
Sing a song always

# 323
# FIT 2 WALK RIGHT

God is:
Rich, Merciful
Great, Loving
Life Giving
Relationship Building
Master Craftsman
Producer
Creator
Purposeful Planner

GOD IS:
Rich in Mercy
Great in love
Giver of Life
Together with Christ
Our Producer
Our Creator
Our Ordainer
Purpose Driven and
Sustainer

Lord, teach us how to walk.

*Ephesians 2:4, 5, 10*

# 324
# FIT 2 WATCH GOD WORK
## with Covid-19

Repairing our families
Restoring our faith
Reviving our church

Renewing our love
Regaining our hope
Rebuilding our marriage

Reading God's Word
Remembering His promises
Readjusting our priorities

Refocusing our purpose
Recalling His peace
Removing our fears
Reconnecting with friends

All things work together
for good

*Romans 8:28*

# 324a
# PEANUT BUTTER ON TOAST

### Psalm 5:11
*Spread your protection over them, that those who
love your name may rejoice in you.*

One of my favorite snacks is toast made from 12-grain wheat bread,
spread with peanut butter. I like to make sure the peanut butter covers the
entire piece of bread, right to the very edge and I take great effort to make
that happen.

That picture of my toast covered from crust to crust with peanut butter
is what comes to my mind when I read Psalm 5:11. God's protection is
spread over those who love His name and find their joy in following Him.
He covers every nook and cranny of my life with nothing left unprotected.
Because I love His name, I am reassured from this verse that I am fully
covered, fully protected.

Psalm 139:7-12 gives us a summary of how God spreads His protection over His children when the psalmist says, "Where can I go from your Spirit? Where can I flee from your presence? If I go up to the heavens, you are there; if I make my bed in the depths, you are there. If I rise on the wings of the dawn, if I settle on the far side of the sea, even there your hand will guide me, your right hand will hold me fast. If I say, "Surely the darkness will hide me and the light become night around me," even the darkness will not be dark to you; the night will shine like the day, for darkness is as light to you."

# Index

# ACKNOWLEDGEMENTS

For me, Russ, this book was a big undertaking. I had a multitude of poems that needed to be organized. There are many people who helped make this book a reality.

God has been my refuge, strength and hope. Without Him, I would have nothing to write.

My parents gave me a love for the Word of God that has not dimmed through the years.

My wife inspired and challenged me to put my poems into book form and then created an index to help make the poems more accessible. She authored the devotional thoughts throughout the book to add insight.

Isaac gathered and organized my poems into a workable electronic format.

My friends prayed with me that this book would happen.

Xulon Press provided support and enthusiasm that kept me going.

Thank you. You have all helped make part of my dream come true. The rest of the dream is my prayer that the result of this effort will be a source of blessing and encouragement to anyone who reads this book.

Daniel used his excellent photography skills for our photograph on the cover.

# About the Authors

Russ is a retired quality engineer who has been writing poetry for almost all of his life, often writing in response to his Bible reading and meditation. Most of his poems are a reflection on the need to grow consistently stronger in one's Christian walk, reflected in the theme of fitness in the poem titles. In recent years, he has used his poetry to develop a ministry of encouragement by way of email. He writes almost every day and, on some days, more than one poem.

Russ's poems reflect his life mission statement:
SEEK THE LORD
AND FIND
PEACE IN HIS PRESENCE
HOPE IN HIS PROMISE
JOY IN HIS PROVISION

SEEK THE LORD
> I choose to seek the Lord with all my heart, with all my mind and with all my strength
> Seeking first the kingdom of God
> Seeking the Lord while He may be found
> Drawing near to God and He will be drawing near to me

FIND PEACE IN HIS PRESENCE
> Thou wilt keep him in perfect peace whose mind is stayed on Thee
> Great peace have they which love Thy law
> My peace I give you
> I will begin to have the "peace of God that passes all understanding"

HOPE IN HIS PROMISE
> I will never leave you nor forsake you

I go to prepare a place for you
Christ in you the hope of glory
I will have a "hope that maketh not ashamed, for he that hath this hope
purifieth himself"

## JOY IN HIS PROVISION

Ask and receive that your joy may be full
God gives us all things that pertain to life and godliness
Exceedingly, abundantly, above all
I will begin to rejoice in whatever the Lord provides, giving thanks for
Everything in the name of the Lord, for my God shall supply all my
need "according" to His riches, not out of His riches

Jo Ann retired as a seminary librarian, having previously served as a missionary and Bible teacher. She has been journaling thoughts from her daily devotional times for many years and uses her journaling to write outlines for Bible studies.

Russ and Jo Ann are both transplanted Yankees who have lived more than half their lives in the South, making them "Southerners by choice," as Russ likes to put it. They live in Lexington, South Carolina.

CPSIA information can be obtained
at www.ICGtesting.com
Printed in the USA
LVHW022022240521
688348LV00015B/636